UBU REPERTORY THEATER PUBLICATIONS

Individual plays:

* *Swimming Pools at War* by Yves Navarre, 1982.
* *Night Just Before the Forest* and *Struggle of the Dogs and the Black*
by Bernard-Marie Koltès, 1982.
The Fetishist by Michel Tournier, 1983. (Out of print).
* *The Office* by Jean-Paul Aron, 1983.
* *Far From Hagondange* and *Vater Land, the Country of our Fathers*
by Jean-Paul Wenzel, 1984.
Deck Chairs by Madeleine Laïk, 1984. (Out of print).
The Passport and *The Door* by Pierre Bourgeade, 1984.
(Out of print).
The Showman by Andrée Chedid, 1984. (Out of print).
* *Madame Knipper's Journey to Eastern Prussia* by Jean-Luc Lagarce,
1984.
Family Portrait by Denise Bonal, 1985; new edition, 1992.
Passengers by Daniel Besnehard, 1985. (Out of print).
* *Cabale* by Enzo Cormann, 1985.
Enough is Enough by Protais Asseng, 1986.
Monsieur Thôgô-gnini by Bernard Dadié, 1985.
The Glorious Destiny of Marshal Nnikon Nniku by Tchicaya U Tam'si,
1986.
Parentheses of Blood by Sony Labou Tansi, 1986.
Intelligence Powder by Kateb Yacine, 1986.
The Sea Between Us by Denise Chalem, 1986.
Country Landscapes by Jacques-Pierre Amette, 1986.
Nowhere and *A Man with Women* by Reine Bartève, 1987.
The White Bear by Daniel Besnehard, 1992.
The Best of Schools by Jean-Marie Besset, 1992.
Jock by Jean-Louis Bourdon, 1992.
A Tempest by Aimé Césaire, 1993 (new edition).
The Free Zone and *The Workroom* by Jean-Claude Grumberg, preface
by Michael R. Marrus, 1993.

Ubu Repertory Theater: 1982-1992, A bilingual illustrated history
with personal statements by various playwrights and theater
personalities, 1992.

* *Distributed by Ubu Repertory Theater, 15 West 28th Street, New York,
NY 10001. All other titles distributed by Theatre Communications Group,
355 Lexington Avenue, New York, NY 10017.*

Anthologies

Afrique I: New plays from the Congo, Ivory Coast, Senegal and Zaire, including *The Daughter of the Gods* by Abdou Anta Kâ, *Equatorium* by Maxime N'Debeka, *Lost Voices* by Diur N'Tumb, *The Second Ark* by Sony Labou Tansi, and *The Eye* by Bernard Zadi Zaourou. Preface by George C. Wolfe. 1987. (Out of print).

The Paris Stage: Recent Plays: *A Birthday Present for Stalin* by Jean Bouchaud, *The Rest Have Got It Wrong* by Jean-Michel Ribes, *The Sleepless City* by Jean Tardieu, *Trumpets of Death* by Tilly, and *The Neighbors* by Michel Vinaver. Preface by Catherine Temerson and Françoise Kourilsky. 1988.

Plays by Women: An International Anthology: *A Picture Perfect Sky* by Denise Bonal, *Jocasta* by Michèle Fabien, *The Girls from the Five and Ten* by Abla Farhoud, *You Have Come Back* by Fatima Gallaire-Bourega, and *Your Handsome Captain* by Simone Schwarz-Bart. Preface by Catherine Temerson and Françoise Kourilsky. 1988, 1991.

Gay Plays: An International Anthology: *The Function* by Jean-Marie Besset, *A Tower Near Paris* and *Grand Finale* by Copi, *Return of the Young Hippolytus* by Hervé Dupuis, *Ancient Boys* by Jean-Claude van Itallie, and *The Lives and Deaths of Miss Shakespeare* by Liliane Wouters. Preface by Catherine Temerson and Françoise Kourilsky. 1989, 1991.

Theater and Politics: An International Anthology: *Black Wedding Candles for Blessed Antigone* by Sylvain Bemba, *A Season in the Congo* by Aimé Césaire, *Burn River Burn* by Jean-Pol Fargeau, *Olympe and the Executioner* by Wendy Kesselman and *Mephisto*, adapted from Klaus Mann by Ariane Mnouchkine. Preface by Erika Munk. 1990.

Afrique II: New Plays from Madagascar, Mauritania and Togo including *The Legend of Wagadu as Seen by Sia Yatabere* by Moussa Diagana, *The Crossroads* by Josué Kossi Efoui, *The Herd* by Charlotte-Arrisoa Rafenomanjato, *The Prophet and the President* by Jean-Luc Raharimanana and *The Singing Tortoise* and *Yevi's Adventures in Monsterland* by Sénouvo Agbota Zinsou. Preface by Henry Louis Gates, Jr. 1991.

Jean-Claude Grumberg

THE
FREE ZONE

and

THE
WORKROOM

Translated from the French
by **Catherine Temerson**

Preface by
Michael R. Marrus

Ubu Repertory Theater Publications
NEW YORK

Ubu Repertory Theater Publications
Françoise Kourilsky
Catherine Temerson
General Editors

Printed in the United States of America, 1993.
Library of Congress Catalogue Card Number: 93-060152
ISBN: 0-913745-39-1

Distributed by Theatre Communications Group,
355 Lexington Avenue, New York, NY 10017

Price: $12.95

The publication of this book was made possible by a grant from the Grand Marnier Foundation and Michel Roux.

CONTENTS

PREFACE

I see how dumbfounded everyone is when I am asked for news and when I have to reply in agony that Monsieur Roussetzki is deported.

Everyone knows how terrible that is! And me, I didn't want to believe it, but the facts are there. If he had been treated humanely he would be able to write, to correspond with his family...

As a Frenchwoman I appeal to your ministry and shout out my indignation. Where is my husband? What has become of my husband?

Letter to Marshal Pétain, 1943

Like Madame Roussetzki who wrote this letter, the seamstress Simone in Jean-Claude Grumberg's play, *The Workroom,* understood the word "deported" in a very special sense. "[My husband] is not here," she tells a co-worker in 1945. "He's been deported." Simone's husband, we learn, was one of the many thousands of foreign Jews rounded up by French police and dispatched "to an unknown destination," as the official cover story had it. "They weren't after me," Simone explains, "they were after my husband. He wasn't home, so they took me and the kids to the station instead. The eleventh precinct...The police captain, also very nice, looked at my papers and told me to go home. He said they didn't have orders to arrest French citizens..."

In all, we now know from the meticulously compiled German lists, at least 75,721 Jews were sent from France to extermination camps in Poland, mainly Auschwitz. After a few days' journey without food or water, the vast majority were gassed upon arrival and their bodies burned; the rest were put to work under conditions that few survived for long. Of these deportees, two-thirds were foreigners, over 6,000 were under the age of thirteen, 2,000 were under six, and 8,700 were sixty years of age or over. What is unusual about France, and what makes the issue such a difficult one in the French historical consciousness, is that these deportations occurred with the substantial assistance of the French government in Vichy, the French administration, and the French police. Alone among European regimes with the exception of that in Bulgaria, the French handed over Jews from a zone unoccupied by German military forces — "the free zone," as Grumberg refers to it, using the terminology of the time — to the Nazis for dispatch "to the East."

Understandably, the French reflect uneasily on this dark moment in their nation's history — just as Jean-Claude Grumberg's characters, Jews and non-Jews, victims and bystanders, rescuers and rescued, seek unsatisfactorily to come to terms with it. During the war, as the letter which precedes this preface suggests, much was still obscure. What was the destination of the dreaded deportation convoys? Were the rumors of gassings true? "What has become of my husband?" Madame Roussetzki implores, — suggesting that she hoped against hope that he was still alive. "What more do they want from us?" asks Monsieur Apfelbaum, one of the hunted Jews in *The Free Zone;* it is the question of a man who has not fully grasped the essence of Vichy and Nazi racial persecution.

Until the Liberation, many managed to put the fate of the Jews out of their minds. In the disorder of the immediate postwar period, with so many others returning from a hard time in Germany, surviving Jewish deportees found but a small place in the French public consciousness.

When deportees first returned from their ordeal, some misperceptions about what happened to the Jews were heightened. As Annette Wieviorka has pointed out in an important new book, French may be the only language in which the term "deportee" as applied to the Second World War came to refer not to people forcibly expelled from their country, but rather to people sent to a Nazi concentration camp. As such, the word designated not only Jews, taken away to be murdered, but also captured resistance fighters, hostages, and miscellaneous anti-Nazis; it was even applied to forced laborers, sent to Germany to work for the Nazi war machine.[1] In 1945, nearly sixty percent of the "political" deportees actually returned to France — some 37,000 who managed to survive concentration camps in Germany. The more than 900,000 French prisoners of war held until the German collapse also returned home, together with over 700,000 forced laborers. These returnees reached France in the full glare of publicity. Arriving with great fanfare by train at the Paris Gare d'Orsay or by bus or airplane at Le Bourget, they sometimes passed through the Hôtel Lutetia in Paris, and frequently found themselves celebrated in the media as national heroes whose ordeals were part of the national war effort. Compared to these the "racial" deportees, Jews who somehow remained alive after the death camps in the East as well as unspeakable trials at the end of the war, were a tiny and insignificant handful — a pitiful 2,500, or about three percent of those originally taken away. Theirs was hardly a joyous return, and their special victimization was scarcely noticed or ill-understood. There were too few of them to count for much and the stories they had to tell were not always what their audience wanted to hear.

(1) Annette Wieviorka, *Déportation et génocide: entre la mémoire et l'oubli.* (Paris: Plon, 1992), 29.

With humanity and compassion, as well as with great skill, Jean-Claude Grumberg portrays one part of their experiences, steeping us in the lives of ordinary men and women — a welcome relief, if my own reading is any indication, for those of us who spend too much time reading about heads of government and important administrators, those who made the decisions that tracked down Jews in *The Free Zone*. Grumberg's plays are part of a broader process now under way in France of revisiting and reevaluating the country's wartime past, and attempting to put into perspective the murderous victimization of an unsuspecting and defenseless minority. "I don't want to have anything to do with the dead," protests Léon, owner of the workroom, himself one of the hunted during the war, speaking in some sense for an entire society. We know, however, that he cannot get the dead out of his mind. Neither, Jean-Claude Grumberg's plays suggest, should we.

MICHAEL R. MARRUS
January 1993

Jean-Claude Grumberg

THE
FREE ZONE

Translated from the French
by **Catherine Temerson**

Ubu Repertory Theater Publications
NEW YORK

The Free Zone, in Catherine Temerson's translation, had its American premiere at Ubu Repertory Theater, 15 West 28th Street, New York, N Y 10001, on March 9th, 1993.

Director:..**Françoise Kourilsky**
Set Designer:.......................................**Watoku Ueno**
Lighting Designer:..............................**Greg MacPherson**
Costume Designer:..............................**Carol Ann Pelletier**
Composer and Sound Designer:...........**Genji Ito**

CAST, IN ORDER OF APPEARANCE

Maury...**Bernie Passeltiner**
Lea..**Polly Adams**
Mrs. Schwartz....................................**Mildred Clinton**
Mauricette...**Patti Perkins**
Henri...**Oren J. Sofer**
Simon...**Ronald Guttman**
Maury's Grandson.............................**J.D. Hyman**
Mr. Apfelbaum..................................**Michael Ingram**
Maury's Daughter-in-law...................**Jodie Lynne McClintock**
Policeman # 1...................................**Dan Daily**
Policeman # 2...................................**Ian Cohen**
The Young German............................**Ivan Borodin**

Produced by **Ubu Repertory Theater**
Françoise Kourilsky, *Artistic Director.*

INTRODUCTION

After writing *Dreyfus,* a play about Polish Jews in the thirties set in an imagined, reinvented Poland—a mythical Poland drawn from family narratives and readings by an author who had never set foot there himself—I wrote *The Workroom,* attempting to portray those same Jews, now French and survivors, adrift in post-war Paris.

The Workroom was conceived like an autobiographical novel; these were people and places I had known and frequented, loved and hated. At the time I was asked why I had written one play about the pre-war period and another about the post-war period, but none set during the war. I had no answer except that it seemed too difficult, too indecent, for a writer like me to stage the catastrophe. More specifically, in Belgium, during a discussion following a performance of *The Workroom,* a young woman asked me how I felt about vengeance. I didn't really understand her question.

As soon as the performances of *The Workroom* were over, I started writing *The Free Zone,* blindly, as though I had something urgent to finish. But soon I had to acknowledge that I wasn't up to the task. I had the characters and the period; I knew the anti-Jewish legislation by heart, had a vague outline and the locations in mind, yet I wasn't up to it.

During the last ten years I wrote many other things, but I had one main goal, one sole desire, one overriding project: *The Free Zone.* The period, during which I had been only semi-conscious, eluded me. Born in 1939, I had lived in hiding in the free zone throughout the war, clutching my older brother's hand. Yet the free zone, situated between the imagined Poland of *Dreyfus* and the all-too-vivid workroom of my childhood, seemed inaccessible.

Moreover, as in *The Workroom*, I wanted to show my Jews living as they must among others. I wanted to show them without lauding them—Kafka said it's impossible to laud what is ours—but even more importantly, without humiliating them. I wanted to honor simultaneously their courage and cowardliness, their blindness and perspicacity.

Of course, I also had to set the action in the most untheatrical location imaginable—in the remote countryside—in a nondescript house lost in the fields, far from the drama and madness, far from Drancy and the Vél d'Hiv, on the other side—the good side—of the demarcation line, far, far away as well from the spot where people crossed from one zone to the other. It had to be set in the kind of place where nothing happens and people wait. The kind of place where every decision is painful and every word a rehash, echo, or rumor.

It took me ten years to write the play, or rather it took me ten years to get used to the idea that it would be what it is and not an all-inclusive statement on the crime, chaos, misfortune and desolation. It would remain a hybrid product, trapped between laughter and tears, derision and real-life memories which someone—I don't even really know who—had whispered to me and shared with me when I was a child. It took me ten years to accept the idea that it would speak so inadequately on the subject of vengeance—a desire forever unfulfilled because it is unfulfillable.

It also took me ten years to realize that I had to write the play in two languages, French and Yiddish, two languages which would become one on stage through the magic of theater. The Yiddish lines, therefore, will simply be spoken in French, with no accent if possible. The characters who are not supposed to understand Yiddish simply won't, while the public will. This device struck me as the only way of avoiding ethnicity and confidentiality.

It was the ban on speaking Yiddish, more than the language itself, that had to be at the heart of the action—the danger Yiddish represented and how this danger weighed on those who knew no other language and those who accompanied them.

Hence Simon, the head of the family, a person ungifted for giving orders, forbids the others from speaking Yiddish right from the Prologue. So be it.

The author—it's part of his craft—finds a gimmick, a trick, which will allow compliance to Simon's justified injunction and yet permit Mrs. Schwartz to express herself though she only desires to do so in Yiddish.

JEAN-CLAUDE GRUMBERG
May 17, 1989

*Since he was unjustly condemned, he should be all-virtuous.
He is innocent, which is already no small matter.*

BERNARD LAZARE

They all mock me, for as soon as I speak, I shout.

JEREMIAH

Spread out on a tulle curtain is a naive and idyllic landscape of the French countryside like an advertisement vaunting the peacefulness of Vichy France's slogan, "Work, Family and Country". This vision is accompanied by overidealized country sounds. Gradually darkness falls, the wind picks up, the tulle quivers, the sounds change, and a storm threatens the peaceful hamlet submerged in greenery. Through the tulle we begin to make out the rustic interior of a large room which was, in its day, the kitchen and main room of a country house now abandoned and rather dilapidated. A large bed, tilted like the floor, makes it possible to imagine that in pressing circumstances the room could be used as a place to sleep.

PROLOGUE

After a moment's resistance, the door opens as the tulle curtain rises. A man appears in the evening light holding two hurricane lamps which he sets down on the table. Following him is a group of five people: Lea, a woman in her forties carrying a suitcase and a purse; her sister Mauricette, just visibly pregnant, and their mother, Mrs. Schwartz, who is holding Mauricette's arm. Henri, Mrs. Schwartz's grandchild and nephew to Lea and Mauricette, follows; he looks older than his thirteen-odd years. He is dragging several suitcases and bundles as Simon, the head of the family, struggles at the doorway with the rest of the luggage. They are dressed in a motley array of city clothes. Maury, the owner of the premises and the first to have entered, is wearing his peasant's best. After setting the lamps down and lighting them, he turns from right to left, arms slightly spread, before speaking.

MAURY: This is it, if it'll do... *(He goes to loosen and push open a wooden shutter.)* Dampness warps the wood.

> *Simon exudes enthusiasm while catching his breath. Like Maury, he bustles about, murmuring.*

SIMON: This is great, isn't it? Great.

> *None of the others responds. Maury blows dust off the table and wipes the top with his velvet-clad forearms.*

LEA: *(hastily)* Please don't. I'll do it.

MAURY: *(still wiping)* If I'd known I'd have asked the son's missis.

The mother starts coughing. Mauricette cautiously taps her on the back. Her mother angrily pushes her away and wipes her mouth with her handkerchief.

THE MOTHER: What are we doing here?

MAURICETTE: Nothing, just spending the night, that's all.

THE MOTHER: Here?

MAURICETTE: Where else?

THE MOTHER: In the bowels of the earth, a hole in hell. You know I can't stand dust.

She clears her throat. Simon, extremely embarrassed, approaches, glaring at them. In response Mauricette leads her mother away. Simon, smiling uncomfortably, mumbles to Maury.

SIMON: Please excuse them, they still talk to each other in "Alsatian"... An old habit.

MAURY: We have a dialect here too. *(Pointing to the bed)* One big bed, two small ones in the other room. We can get some hay for the kid.

He laughs. The kid has already dozed off, seated on a suitcase and buried in an oversized man's coat. Simon points to him, indicating the hay will be unnecessary. Mauricette has taken one of the hurricane lamps and led her mother to the adjoining room. They can be heard arguing as her mother persistently coughs.

MAURY: *(still surveying the premises)* There's kitchenware in the chest. Not so long ago, in 1940, we took in some refugees, Northerners...

SIMON: *(solemnly)* Mr.... Maury, I would really like to...

MAURY: *(cutting him off with a gesture)* Alsatians. My father took some in in 1914. Not here. In the house below, and he even had to put some up at the town hall.

SIMON: Oh good.

MAURY: And you, you're from where?

SIMON: Us? Alsace. We're from Alsace.

MAURY: Where in Alsace?

SIMON: We've just come from Paris, but we're from Alsace.

MAURY: Strasbourg?

SIMON: *(gesturing with his hand)* Further east.

MAURY: Further east is Germany!

SIMON: *(laughing)* Right, right, I see you know your geography, that's unusual... A small village, a small town, east of Strasbourg.

> *Maury turns toward Lea who is standing at the doorway of the adjoining room.*

MAURY: Are you hungry?

SIMON: *(instantly protesting)* No, no...

LEA: If you have some bread or anything for the kid and...

She points to the adjoining room where her sister and mother are.

MAURY: Bread and apples, is that O.K.?

SIMON: Of course, of course. Apples are always welcome, hungry or not.

MAURY: And I'll see if I can dig up some blankets for you.

He exits. As soon as the door closes, Simon rushes into the adjoining room and yells.

SIMON: No more Yiddish! No more Yiddish! No more! Is that understood? *(He re-enters and glares menacingly at Lea who is sitting on a suitcase...)* How many times? How many times?

LEA: *(ignoring the comment and very calm)* He seems nice?

SIMON: Of course, to Alsatians. Everyone's nice to Alsatians... *(He nudges the kid dozing on the suitcase.)* Get up, kid, we've arrived.

HENRI: *(in his sleep)* Have we crossed the demarcation line, uncle?

SIMON: *(helping him)* Yes, we've crossed. Yes. Come, climb up here. You'll see Montmartre. *(He helps him to stretch out on the table, removes his shoes and covers him with a large man's overcoat.)* Sleep tight, nightie night.

The kid glances around.

HENRI: Where are we?

SIMON: *(unable to repress a sense of pride, mumbles)* The "free zone", the "free zone". Go to sleep.

> *Lea kisses Henri and covers him up. The child moans and curls up under the overcoat. His boots, on the floor next to the table, are well worn from hours of walking. He is exhausted. Lea's sigh is also telling. Blackout.*

> *The tulle curtain might be lowered briefly but the French countryside would now be pictured at the center of a map of France divided into the occupied and non-occupied zones.*

SCENE 1

The room is in semi-darkness. The sounds of the countryside are heard, then the roar of a train that seems to cut across the room and the bed where Lea and Simon are resting. Simon sits up, distraught, looks around and then drops back down on his makeshift pillow. He feels oppressed. And then silence; for the city dweller, the haunting silence of country nights. Simon and Lea are lying back to back, each trying to sleep.

LEA: *(murmurs after a time)* Are you sleeping?

SIMON: No. And you?

LEA: Me neither.

Silence.

SIMON: The train woke me up.

LEA: Train? What train?

SIMON: The train.

LEA: There wasn't any train. *(Pause.)* I wasn't sleeping.

SIMON: You were sleeping if you didn't hear it.

LEA: *(after a pause, confidently)* I'm telling you, there wasn't any train. *(Silence, then Lea continues.)* There's no station.

Silence.

SIMON: Between stations trains roll, don't they?

Silence. Back to back, they try to sleep. Suddenly Simon lights the lamp next to the bed.

LEA: Turn it off! What are you doing? You're crazy!

SIMON: I hear noises.

He gets up.

LEA: Trains, noises. You'll be hearing voices next.

Simon walks around the room, acquainting himself with the surroundings. The hastily-abandoned, half-opened luggage gives the large room a precarious look which contrasts with the solid, rustic furniture and the kitchen components—the wood and coal stove, the stone sink and the water pump. Quite independently of the disorder created by the invasion of Simon and his family, the place suggests neglect, as though the building had outlived its time.
Simon is standing next to the big table on top of which Henri is sleeping, curled up in his coat. He holds the light up to the child, awkwardly covering him up. Then he picks up the trousers that had been thrown on the floor and spreads them out carefully over a suitcase.

LEA: Stop, you'll wake him up.

SIMON: *(with admiration)* Amazing, these creatures can sleep anywhere.

LEA: I said stop.

He steps away from the table, seizes a piece of bread and sits down on a suitcase. He nibbles at the bread while talking in a restrained voice.

SIMON: I picked a compartment full of veterans and nuns, and half the time I wound up in the corridor, next to the toilet. He was sick.

LEA: *(also snatching a piece of bread)* He says it was you.

SIMON: Me what?

LEA: You who was sick.

SIMON: Sick from seeing him sick, yes. Silly kid. As it is, I can't stand kids, but this takes the cake! And the idea of passing him off as my son, sorry, but...

LEA: It was your idea.

SIMON: That doesn't necessarily make it a good idea. Frankly, did you look at his face?

LEA: He's cuter than you.

SIMON: Cute! You mean nature hasn't exactly been kind to him. Maybe I'm not cute, but I have the great privilege of looking like any one of these bastards. I can pass, which is essential these days...

LEA: I don't think there's anything special about his looks.

SIMON: Don't get mad... But objectively... Without any makeup, he could pose for the propaganda posters of the General Board for Jewish Affairs. No? The continuing adventures of Henri the Yid in Nono zone...

LEA: Personally, I like his looks. Period.

SIMON: So do I. So do I like his looks, silly. But you've got to admit this year's canons of male beauty aren't exactly in his favor. *(Suddenly he stands up, walks over to the sink, examines the pump that serves as a faucet and grumbles.)* Look, damn it, it drips! It drips, damn it! It's not even a faucet and it drips! *(He sighs and continues.)* Also, I wasn't sure he'd understood our name was Girard and that we were father and son...

LEA: Don't worry, he understands better than you. Now come to bed.

SIMON: *(after a pause)* Anyhow, it all went well.

LEA: Right, it all went well.

SIMON: And your smuggler? Was he O.K.?

LEA: He was O.K. We got across O.K. Everything's O.K. Now come to bed.

SIMON: I won't be able to sleep. *(He is silent, then continues.)* I was so afraid we wouldn't meet up...

LEA: You're the one who didn't want us to cross together.

SIMON: Absolutely. I have a theory about shipping perishable goods. You send several small packages not one big one, that way if one gets lost...

LEA: I know, I know. I've heard all this before. The basket and eggs theory, too, thank you.

SIMON: Anyhow, I never told you to cross the Indre river at night, with your mother, in a row boat.

LEA: What were we supposed to do? Swim across in broad daylight? And stop making the floor creak, you'll wake up the whole house.

SIMON: *(repeating)* The house... *(He stands still, listens to the relative silence, then inquires.)* But we're alright here?

LEA: We're fine. Now come to bed.

SIMON: *(slipping into bed)* I won't be able to sleep.

LEA: Lie down, turn on your side and stop talking.

SIMON: *(complying)* If it weren't for the train I'd still be asleep.

LEA: *(sighing)* Get off the train, turn off the light and count sheep. And stop moving, you're keeping me awake. *(Simon stops moving. Pause.)* Please turn off the light.

SIMON: I can't, I'm thinking.

LEA: You can think in the dark.

SIMON: Not me. I'm scared in the dark, especially when I'm thinking.

LEA: *(hardly containing herself)* Turn that off right now, I've had enough monkey-business.

> *He turns off the light. They are left in darkness and relative silence.*

SIMON: Lucky, wasn't it, coming across that guy... Tipped his cap and, how did he put it? "You wouldn't be seeking a refuge for the night?" Refuge. Depends, I said, depends... *(Pause.)* We haven't discussed money yet. He can't charge much, can he, for this hole in the wall?

LEA: No. Now we stop moving and we sleep.

Silence.

SIMON: *(mumbling after a spell)* Lea? *(She doesn't answer.)* You think there are mice?

LEA: *(almost sitting up as she restrains herself from screaming)* Simon!

SIMON: Because I hear noises, dear.

LEA: Will you stop, please!

Relative silence again.

SIMON: *(whispering after a spell)* Lea!

LEA: Now what?

SIMON: Mind if I move? My arm is like stuck under my knee.

LEA: *(sighing)* Move, don't move, but stop bothering me, damn it!

SIMON: *(after a pause)* O.K., this is it, I'm moving. Hang on, mate!

She sighs. The bed creaks as he turns over, then back again, and finally clasps her in one fell swoop. She instantly pushes him away.

LEA: You crazy? *(Silently, he hugs her again, closer and closer. Lea pushes him away.)* You're crazy. Leave me alone!

SIMON: *(hugging her even more while she pushes him away)* Make up your mind: you said move and when I do you yell.

LEA: *(still pushing him away, determined)* You crazy, with the kid sleeping on the table over there!

SIMON: But he's sleeping and it's dark?

The bed creaks again.

LEA: *(panic-stricken)* Stop, you'll wake up mama.

She has extricated herself and is out of bed.

SIMON: *(defeated)* Mama...

LEA: *(standing next to the bed)* Really, do you think this is the right moment?

SIMON: *(turning away)* With you it's never the right moment. There's always mama. *(She goes over to the door that gives out on the countryside, opens it, and pushes back the heavy wooden shutter.)* Now what are you doing?

LEA: Getting a breath of fresh air, if you don't mind. *(The brilliance and coolness of the night fill the room. From the doorstep)* It's still the dead of night.

SIMON: You'll catch cold.

LEA: I'm hot.

> *She takes in the air and fans herself as though she were having a hot flash.*

SIMON: *(complaining)* Chilling yourself when you're overheated! That's all we need!

LEA: It's so beautiful.

SIMON: Wait till you're sick like a dog!

LEA: *(repeating)* So beautiful...

SIMON: I heard you. Shut it. I'm freezing.

LEA: The stars.

SIMON: We had stars in Paris too, thank you!

LEA: *(shrugging)* Means clear days ahead...

SIMON: So? Any other hokum? You coming to bed? "Clear days ahead." Sounds like Radio-Paris...

> *Lea half-heartedly shuts the door leaving the shutter open. The brightness of the starry night fills the room, giving it an unreal and eerie quality.*

LEA: Move over to your side...

SIMON: *(moving and grumbling)* And here I thought we were in the free zone...

14

LEA: *(sliding back into bed after a pause)* You know, it's really beautiful...

SIMON: Now what? What is?

LEA: Outside, nature, nighttime, the trees.

SIMON: "Nature, the trees", that's their big pitch and here you are, like a sucker, gobbling it up? "It's really beautiful".

LEA: Their big pitch? What pitch?

SIMON: That: nature, trees, the moon, the stars, the firmament, the gentle breeze, birds, cows, the flora and the fauna, it's all part of their lousy propaganda, their back to nature movement.

LEA: O.K., I see. We'll discuss it in the morning... Good night.

SIMON: O.K., O.K., good n-i-i-i-ght!... They've certainly made progress since 1914. Now, a couple of small punches, a quick armistice, no sooner done and they start waging war on civilians. It's less of a strain on them; less messy for their darling nature. In fact while we're on the subject, take advantage of it and get your fill because, believe me, if we make it, you're not going to see much of nature again... We'll stick to the Boulevard Barbès, between Château-Rouge and Marcadet and we won't budge ever again, except maybe to venture down to the Square d'Anvers on holidays, or to the Gare de l'Est to get a beer at the Café de France...

LEA: You've really lost your marbles. I'm going to sleep, if you don't mind? The "Café de France"...

SIMON: Go on, go to sleep, go to sleep. I'll keep watch!

LEA: Fine, keep watch, but in silence.

SIMON: I won't let any greenery get in here. *(Determined and energetic, Lea straightens out her makeshift pillow, then suddenly stops and remains motionless. Simon notices and responds.)* Now what?

LEA: *(whispering)* You woke up mama!

SIMON: Me?

LEA: Yes, you! Who else? The pope? What with your asinine chatter!

> *The following interchange is heard behind the wall.*

— Mauricette?

— Yes, mamele.

— What time is it?

— Four, five, I don't know. Go to sleep.

— Go to sleep? I should say go to sleep. Mothers tell their daughters to go to sleep, not daughters their mothers.

> *After a pause:*

— Lea, the minute she was in bed, she'd fall asleep, but you, I'd no sooner tell you to sleep, you'd start jumping, jumping around in bed, hop, hop, hop, and you'd scream.

16

And when you'd finally fall asleep, you'd scream in your sleep. The neighbors were terrorized: "Mrs. Schwartz, what's going on in your place?" "It's nothing, just my little Mauricette screaming in her sleep." And your father used to laugh and laugh. Doctor Klein used to say, "It's a case of worms"; your father said, "No, it's a case of nerves". And they would argue!... "Mr. Schwartz, do I tell you how to cut clothes?"

— Go to sleep now, mamele, go to sleep!

> *The mother sings a lullaby. This time, the strains are those of Yiddish, the language the two women are supposed to be speaking. Simon and Lea, motionless, listen intently.*

SIMON: *(suddenly, as though he were waking from a nightmare)* Lea, please.

LEA: What?

SIMON: Tell her not to speak Yiddish anymore, tell her...

> *Lea sighs as the mother's lullaby comes to a climax.*

SIMON: *(almost yelling)* And don't sigh when I talk to you!

> *Silence. The lullaby is over. One senses that the two women on the other side of the wall are listening intently.*

LEA: *(protesting and trying to keep her voice to a whisper)* Simon, at night, in a room, out in the middle of...

SIMON: *(cutting her off)* Night, day, outdoors or indoors, I don't want to hear Yiddish anymore! Is that clear? No more Yiddish! Block it out of your head, forget it exists, get into the habit... *(After a pause)* Is it too much to ask, for God's sake? Just that! *(Lea starts sobbing, her head buried in the bed. Simon retreats.)* Well, fine, fine, very good, we'll discuss it again in Drancy, if they don't separate us. Let's sleep now...

LEA: But even when she keeps quiet you say she keeps quiet like an old Jewish woman...

SIMON: First let her keep quiet, then we'll deal with the rest.

LEA: *(interrupting him)* You say it's even worse when she tries to speak French.

SIMON: Let her use sign language, like deaf-mutes. *(Lea doesn't reply. He continues.)* There was no point in using the name Girard and going to the trouble of getting fake papers. We could've just sat and waited for them in the comfort of home.

LEA: *(getting out of bed)* Put it on!

SIMON: Put what on?

LEA: The light!

SIMON: *(grumbling)* Make up your mind: first it's "turn it off", now it's "put it on". *(Nevertheless, reluctantly he lights the lamp. Lea is dressing.)* What are you doing now?

LEA: I'm getting dressed, as you can see.

SIMON: So I see! What for?

LEA: I'm going for a walk.

Silence.

SIMON: *(approving, then)* If the tobacco shop on Boulevard Barbès is open, do me a favor and get me a couple of packs of plain Caporal tobacco and a packet of Job rolling paper.

LEA: Leave me alone, damn it, with your crummy boulevard and your rolling paper.

SIMON: *(after a pause)* Lea, I can tell you, there's nothing open anywhere within a three-hundred-mile radius, and even during the day they don't serve hot meals... Nothing but home-brewed liqueur and hooch.

LEA: *(next to the door)* I'd rather spend the rest of the night in a pigsty, with the hogs, than stay in bed with you a second longer.

SIMON: Fine, provided the hogs around here accept Jews. Come on, get back into bed. I won't move, I won't say anything about anything anymore, I promise! Besides, I didn't say anything, what's there to say?

LEA: *(suddenly enraged, coming back toward the bed)* What did you expect me to do with her, huh? What was it you wanted?

SIMON: Now what? I don't even know what you're talking about.

LEA: Did you want me to just set off for the free zone with my clown of a husband?...

SIMON: Thanks.

LEA: And leave her all alone in Paris? Or maybe I should've delivered her to the camps at Beaune-la-Rolande or Pithiviers?

SIMON: *(humming)*
"Tout va très bien madame la marquise,
Tout va très bien, tout va très bien,
Pourtant il faut, il faut que l'on vous dise"...
The walls have ears...

LEA: *(ignoring him and continuing)* She has no right to talk, no right to breathe, no right to live anymore. Right?

SIMON: Am I to blame? *(Lea is kicking the packages and bundles, scattering them around the room. She is looking for a shawl or warmer shoes. Simon sits up, watches her briefly and asks:)* What are you doing? Throwing a temper tantrum or dancing the jig?

LEA: Putting things away.

SIMON: *(in a low voice)* Honestly, it's one thing to quietly breathe and another to go around constantly moaning and delivering lectures in Yiddish to goys, particularly if they're in uniform. There's a difference, no?

LEA: Not for her, not for her anymore!

Lea finally finds what she is looking for, bundles herself up and starts to exit.

SIMON: Lea! Pick up a map at the reception desk! In case you get lost, make sure you have the address of the hotel!

LEA: *(at the doorstep)* If you only knew. I don't give a damn about your comments. If you only knew...

SIMON: Don't hesitate to take a taxi back, O.K.?

She exits.

HENRI: *(as Simon turns off the light)* What's wrong with auntie — Simon?

SIMON: What? Nothing, sleep. "Auntie-Simon!"...

HENRI: I have to go...

SIMON: So, what can I do about it?

The kid sits up but is still half asleep.

HENRI: Where's the toilet?

SIMON: Anywhere and everywhere.

HENRI: There's no pottie?

SIMON: No, and no bedside rug...

Henri gets up and gropes his way to the door.

SIMON: *(suddenly)* Henri, put on your galoshes! Don't go catching pneumonia, that's all I need. *(But Henri is already outside, barefoot. Mauricette appears at the doorstep of the adjoining room, lamp in hand.)* You too! It's an epidemic! Straight ahead, please. The ladies' room is vacant.

MAURICETTE: *(crossing the room)* Would you mind keeping your voices down when you quarrel? You've woken up mama.

SIMON: Follow the crowd, as I said. It's straight ahead. You can't miss it.

MAURICETTE: I've been holding back for hours so as not to disturb you.

SIMON: You shouldn't have. The baby might come out with webbed feet. Go, go.

MAURICETTE: *(noticing Lea's absence)* Where's Lea?

SIMON: Gone to the hairdresser's. They have discounts at night here... You know how she is...

> *As she exits she meets Henri who is returning. She kisses him. Henri rushes back under the coat, his teeth chattering.*

HENRI: It's all wet outside.

SIMON: *(grumbling)* Toilets are always like that, especially in the country.

HENRI: *(curled up under his coat)* Lea said it's the dew.

SIMON: What?

HENRI: You know, Simon, Lea is crying out there.

SIMON: Please don't say Lea, say aunt Lea, O.K.?

HENRI: Aunt Lea's crying out there, Simon!

SIMON: That's normal. Nature has stirred her artistic soul. Did you pee?

HENRI: Yes, Simon.

SIMON: Do you feel better?

HENRI: *(holding back a giggle)* Yes, Simon.

SIMON: Proves that it's still functioning. When you can pee O.K. means everything's O.K. Now, go to sleep, kid, sleep...

> *Suddenly roosters can be heard calling to each other in the distance. The Yiddish lullaby breaks out again in the adjoining room. Simon pulls the blanket over his head. Blackout.*

SCENE 2

It is broad daylight. Light floods the room from the half-open door. We can guess from the shape on the bed that Simon is buried under the blankets. Henri has spread his notebooks and textbooks out on the table. Along the wall is the straw mat on which he now sleeps. Mrs. Schwartz is dozing, seated by the door on a straw-bottomed chair with armrests. Every once in a while she raises her head, glances around, and suddenly raises her arm as though she were chasing flies away. Henri is engrossed reciting his lesson in an undertone and peering into his notebook to check himself, as he paces in small steps diagonally across the room.

HENRI: Vercingetorix, chieftain of Avernes... Avernes? *(He verifies.)* Arvernes. Chieftain of Arvernes... first personified the spirit of the French people. For a moment he thought victory was his, but Gallic improvisational skills were forced to submit to the organized Roman forces. Vercingetorix capitulated at Alesia in 52 B.C. "Since fate is against us, I offer myself to you," he said to his companions, "appease the Romans with my death, or by delivering me live." They delivered him live. Caesar had him executed after displaying him around Rome in triumph, chained to his chariot. In A.D. 450 the Huns, led by Attila, God's scourge, were repelled outside Lutetia, today Paris, by Saint Genevieve who organized the city's defense. Thirty years later, there was the victory at Tolbiac over the Visigoths and the Burgundans... the Burgundians... owed to Clovis who, true to his vow on the battlefield, was baptized in Reims by Saint Remy. Thanks to Genevieve and Clovis, Western civilization was saved from extinction which would have been the inevitable consequence of a Barbarian victory. Equally menacing was the threat of the Moors who, in the name of Mohammed, wished to extend their conquest of the Iberian Peninsula to Gaul. Charles Martel repulsed their forces at Poitiers in A.D. 732, thereby rescuing our Christian civilization. During the Middle Ages, in A.D. 1214, as the unification of France progressed, King Philip Augustus triumphed over the Northern lords at Bouvines. His battle cry was "Montjoie Saint Denis!" *(He stops and in a fierce but still low voice, articulates:)* "Montjoie Saint Denis!" *(He stops to caracole and draws an imaginary sword with which he slices the air. Then he begins pacing again.)* The outstanding event of that period, however, was the Hundred Years' War whose sole object was to drive back the English who wanted hegemony and their king to rule our country... hegemony? *(Pause. He thinks, then continues.)* In response, a simple shepherdess, Joan of Arc, raised her standard. She delivered Orleans in A.D. 1429. But the English, supported by bribed traitors, captured Joan of Arc and burned her at the stake in Rouen in A.D. 1431. Thus did France forge her unity, century by century, thanks to the sacrifice of her sons and daughters. Alas, once consolidated and unified by a succession of kings, France, more than any other nation, was torn by fratricidal strife. Yet when the need arose, France was able to rally her forces and save her integrity. "Today, I am giving myself to France to alleviate her misfortune". With these words Marshal Pétain, the victor of Verdun, addressed the French people, June 17, 1940, and promised to lead the government of a defeated France. Not since the valorous chieftain of Avernes... Arvernes... who, on an autumn day in Alesia decided to give himself over to his conqueror to safeguard his people's unity, can a comparable chivalrous spirit be found in the midst of defeat.

As he concludes he is facing the door and discovers a five-or six-year-old child who has silently entered moments earlier and is squatting, delighted, as he listens at the doorstep. Silence. The two children stare at each other.

THE CHILD: *(asking, finally, in a low voice)* What are you playing?

HENRI: *(also in a low voice)* I'm studying.

THE CHILD: What?

HENRI: My lessons.

Solemnly, he goes up to the table, puts down his history notebook and picks up another. The child watches in fascination. Renewed silence.

THE CHILD: *(finally, still in a low voice)* Is your daddy my grandpa's Jew?

Henri brings his index finger to his lips to silence him, then explains in a low voice:

HENRI: No, my father isn't here.

THE CHILD: *(whispering)* Where is he?

HENRI: *(absorbed in his notebooks)* I don't know.

THE CHILD: *(after a pause)* Mine is a prisoner of the Germans.

HENRI: Well, so is mine.

THE CHILD: *(surprised)* Oh? *(Silence.)* And do you think they're far away?

HENRI: *(after staring at him)* Do you go to school?

THE CHILD: Not yet, I'm too little. *(Silence.)* Do you pray a lot?

HENRI: Me? What for?

THE CHILD: So your daddy will come back?

> *Silence. Henri seems absorbed by his notebooks and books. Prolonged silence. The child then places a letter on the table.*

THE CHILD: Here, my grandpa sent me up with this.

> *He exits, very proud. On the way, he stops momentarily right in front of Mrs. Schwartz and stares at her. She suddenly sticks out her tongue and waves her hands around her ears. Torn between laughter and fear, the child runs away hastily. Mrs. Schwartz falls back into her apathetic state. On the bed, Simon turns over under the covers, suppressing a coughing fit. Henri is momentarily engrossed in his books, then he reaches for the letter and reads it in an undertone, again pacing up and down.*

HENRI: To the attention of Mr. Maury. Re: lost parcels. This is to inform you that the addressees were transferred from Royallieu-près-Compiègne to Drancy, and consequently the last parcels you sent were delayed in the forwarding process. However they are neither lost nor spoiled. The addressees will await your future shipments in Drancy. Kindly use the enclosed labels to facilitate dispatching. Regulations allow no more than one five-kilogram parcel every two weeks and no perishable goods. Sincerely. (*Henri stops still for a moment, then walks briskly up to the bed where his uncle is lying. He shakes him several times; his uncle groans from under the covers.*) Simon! Simon!

SIMON: What is it?

HENRI: (*placing the letter on the blanket*) They're in Drancy.

SIMON: (*his head emerging briefly*) Drancy? (*He remains still for a minute, unshaven and hair disheveled. Henri returns to the table and picks up his history notebook. Simon glances at the letter, slides it under his pillow and asks:*) Have the women returned?

HENRI: No.

SIMON: (*coughing softly*) I hope they'll bring me some cough syrup.

> *He vanishes back under the covers, coughing. Henri starts pacing again; for a moment he is silent, then he begins mumbling.*

HENRI: Vercingetorix, chieftain of Avernes...

> *Blackout.*

SCENE 3

The interior of the house is in semi-darkness; outside it is broad daylight. There is a knock at the door. Simon emerges from under the blanket. The knocking becomes more insistent. He sits up, terrified, unshaven. He hesitates and lifts his hand up to his head. The knocking becomes even more insistent. He rushes over to a window and tries to look outside without being seen. Then he positions himself next to the door so that he will be hidden when it opens. At that moment the door yields to the weight of a man who walks in puzzled by the darkness.

APFELBAUM: Mr. Zilberberg, it's me, Ludovic Apfelbaum, from rue Doudeauville.

SIMON: *(from where he is standing)* Not Zilberberg, Girard. And not in Yiddish, in French, please!

He appears.

APFELBAUM: Mr. Zilberberg, that the other children, little bastards and so on, sons of bastards and so on, spend their time calling my Daniel... well, O.K., what can I do? That's life, huh? But that your kid, yours, it really...it...*(He presses his solar plexus, his mouth suddenly dry, but affirms vehemently:)* Each father is responsible for each word, bad or good, that comes out of the mouth of his child!

SIMON: *(also very loudly trying to contain the onslaught)* First of all, he isn't my child.

APFELBAUM: *(interrupting him)* Mr. Zilberberg, please, no wisecracks, eh, no wisecracks. We've known each other too long. Let's converse like citizens who are conscious of

29

their rights and duties, please.

SIMON: *(barking finally)* Girard! Say Gi-rard!

APFELBAUM: I'm sorry, but you know, it's useless to change your first name. It's the last name that should be changed, not the first name.

SIMON: Not Gérard, Girard. Simon Girard, that's me: Girard!

APFELBAUM: I also changed to cross the line and everything. They stuck me with an unpronounceable name, Gaillac, Goillac, Guillac or whatever. But here, at the Limoges police headquarters, I registered as Ludovic Apfelbaum; Jewish; French citizen by virtue of the naturalization act; born in Tarnapolsky, Byelorussia; address: rue Doudeauville; et cetera. So my I.D. and ration cards were all issued in my real name. That way I can walk proud on any country road in Haute-Vienne, and even in the border departments, so they told me... But why would I go there? What would I do there? What am I doing here?

SIMON: Here we're in Corrèze, Haute-Vienne is up the hill.

APFELBAUM: Oh, we're in Corrèze?

SIMON: *(enraged, rumaging around the burner and brusquely placing a pot of water on it)* O.K., what's going on? Your son and my nephew got into an argument, and so you come barnstorming in here in the middle of the night?

APFELBAUM: In the middle of the night? It's noon!

SIMON: *(almost yelling)* My nights are difficult!

APFELBAUM: Maybe you think mine are custom-made? His nights are difficult! I get up at seven every day, difficult or not! And I make charcoal.

He raises his hands; they are black.

SIMON: Is this what you came to tell me? You'd like me to stick a rotating neon yellow star on the roof? Just because you registered as Jewish at the police headquarters I should also get picked up?

APFELBAUM: Mr. Gérard, Gilbert or whatever...

SIMON: Girard! Gi-rard!

APFELBAUM: I should be shouting at you, not you at me, after what your son said to mine!

SIMON: He's not my son, damn it, he's my nephew!

APFELBAUM: Your brother's son?

SIMON: No, I don't have a brother, the son of one of my wife's brothers.

APFELBAUM: Sorry, I didn't ask after her. How is she? And... her mother? Daniel told me she was here with you, right?

SIMON: Everyone's fine, thank you. Could we cut the polite small talk?

APFELBAUM: *(without catching his breath, agrees vigorously)*

What can I do? What can I do? The less he eats the fatter he gets. Everyone gets thin, he gets fat. And thin children don't like fat children — why, who knows?... Also, he wears glasses, and children who don't wear glasses hate children who do. And without his glasses, he bumps into things and trips. What can I do? What can I do? And then, yes, true, yes, yes, he's a good student! He barely reads a page and he already knows it. Even without reading it, if he just turns the page, he's got it memorized. In catechism, after three lessons, he's already the best in the class. It's so easy, he says to me, if you knew, papale, the nonsense... O.K., I can't very well say to him, Daniel don't study and you'll be popular, no? And then yes, true, yes, he doesn't like to fight, he doesn't like it and he doesn't know how. Do you?

SIMON: What? Do I what?

APFELBAUM: Know how to fight? Do you know how to fight? I don't. Nor does he. And, besides, yes, he's like me, he's scared. He's scared! So the others take advantage, they make fun of him, they call him... What kind of world is this where you have to know how to fight before they'll respect you, what kind of world is this? *(He suddenly throws a few punches in the air.)* Is this what's called a man? This?

> *Simon watches him, bewildered, while bustling near the stove where the water is boiling.*

SIMON: Would you like some herbal tea, Mr. Apfelbaum? I'm making some for myself anyway.

> *Apfelbaum waves the offer aside with the back of his hand, then continues.*

APFELBAUM: Every evening, I swear, he comes home from

school, every evening he cries. He cries. A strapping kid like him, who already wears a size sixteen shirt and a ten and half size shoe, he cries. What can I do? What can I do?

SIMON: *(pouring a bit of water in two bowls)* And me? What can I do?

APFELBAUM: *(hardly allowing him to finish his sentence, he's grabbed him by the throat, and indifferent to spilling the boiling water, shakes him and yells)* Your son calls a Jewish child a dirty Jew and you ask me what you can do?

SIMON: *(freeing himself)* What did you say? What did you just say? Are you crazy or something?

APFELBAUM: *(suddenly quieted, carefully points to the center of his chest and murmurs)* It pains me terribly, right here, terribly.

> Suddenly he sits down on the edge of the table and presses his hand against his solar plexus. Silence. Simon, not knowing what to say, starts arguing.

SIMON: He's not my... *(He sets down a bowl next to Apfelbaum.)* Here, drink. *(They drink in silence. He breaks the silence.)* His father is you know where...

> Brief silence. They continue drinking.

APFELBAUM: *(putting down the bowl)* If his father is where you say he is, it's up to you to set a good example. And if he comes back from school Saturday at noon and finds you still in bed, don't be surprised if later he turns into a hoodlum!

SIMON: What's that got to do with it? What? First of all, Henri isn't a hoodlum. This is kidstuff all of this.

APFELBAUM: *(rising, pointing a finger, menacing)* Listen to me, Mr. Zilberberg, if your Henri ever calls my Daniel... *(He stops, finger pointing. Simon waits for him to continue. Apfelbaum suddenly lets his arm fall, hunches his shoulders, and presses and releases his solar plexus again.)* What's the world coming to? I ask you, what's the world coming to? My regards to your charming wife and her dear mother. Excuse me for disturbing your sleep. *(He is already standing at the door.)* It's a comfort, isn't it, to talk to someone from the neighborhood from time to time?

> *He exits holding his chest.*

SIMON: *(rushing to put on his trousers over his pajama bottoms and shouting as he buttons them up)* Wait, wait, I'll walk part of the way with you!

> *But Apfelbaum has already vanished. Simon walks back to the center of the room, paces up and down, then rips off his leather belt and strikes it savagely against the mattress while uttering a terrifying cry. Mrs. Schwartz appears from the adjoining room, a coat thrown over her nightgown.*

THE MOTHER: What's going on here?

SIMON: Nothing. I'm airing out the bedding.

> *He strikes again but without violence.*

THE MOTHER: What time is it?

SIMON: Noon.

THE MOTHER: The girls aren't here?

SIMON: No. Would you like a warm drink?

THE MOTHER: I didn't sleep a wink. Why do they stuff their mattresses with nutshells in these parts? Why?

She disappears. Simon remains alone, holding the belt, puzzled. After a pause, he goes into the other room and asks:

SIMON: Herbal tea? No? I made some.

The mother can be heard moaning and turning over in bed.

SIMON: You shouldn't lounge around in bed like this all day! It's exhausting in the end...

THE MOTHER: Where should I go? There isn't even a sidewalk with a bench around here...

While Simon is in the other room, Henri slips into the house, puts down his briefcase and walks toward the door. Simon enters as he's about to exit.

SIMON: (*rushing in as though he had heard him*) Henri!

HENRI: (*from the steps*) I just dropped off my briefcase.

SIMON: Come here.

HENRI: My friends are waiting, Simon.

SIMON: Here! (*Mechanically, he cracks the belt. Henri enters and remains at the doorstep, shoulders hunched, waiting. With difficulty:)* Why'd you do it?

HENRI: Why'd I do what, Simon?

Silence.

SIMON: *(yelling in a low voice)* Apfelbaum! *(Silence. He repeats the question insistently:)* Why?

HENRI: *(after a pause, murmurs)* I don't know.

SIMON: "I don't know" isn't an answer.

HENRI: He hangs around me all the time, I don't like him, he's a leech.

Silence.

SIMON: *(suddenly whipping the belt against the table)* If your father were here he'd kill you. Do you hear me? He'd kill you.

Henri begins to sob.

SIMON: *(retreating)* Don't cry. Don't cry.

HENRI: I can't help it, Simon.

SIMON: From now on, you'll say "Uncle Simon", not "Simon". Yes, Uncle Simon, no Uncle Simon, thank you Uncle Simon, and so on.

HENRI: *(after a while still crying)* I'm miserable, Uncle Simon, miserable. I say things, I don't even know why I say them. *(Silence. Raising his head abruptly)* I don't want to go back to school.

SIMON: You don't want to go back, that's a good one! His lordship doesn't want to go back! You could apologize, no? Would it break your jaw, do you think, to say you're sorry?

HENRI: *(firm)* I want to go back to Paris.

SIMON: He wants to go back to Paris! And what would you do in Paris?

HENRI: I would work.

SIMON: At your age, kids don't work, they go to school.

HENRI: Maybe I would hear from them? Maybe they're back and looking for me?

Silence.

SIMON: First of all, there's no going back to Paris.

HENRI: Why not?

SIMON: Because, because... because it's forbidden.

HENRI: I won't say... I'll say what you told me to say: Alsatian.

SIMON: No, no, no, no sir. If you're lucky enough to be in the free zone, you don't go rushing back into the lion's den! Sorry, no! Anyhow, enough of this nonsense, you're going to pass your exams and get your diploma, and that's that.

HENRI: What for?

SIMON: What for? What do you mean what for? He's asking me what for! *(They remain face to face, then Simon lowers his eyes, puts his belt back on and says:)* Well, O.K., that's it, don't just stand there, your friends are waiting.

HENRI: *(staring at him)* They're not my friends, Uncle Simon, they're not my friends.

> *He stands still, staring at his uncle who begins bustling about near the burner. Blackout.*

SCENE 4

A winter night in 1942. On stage, Mrs. Schwartz, a shawl or blanket tightly wrapped over her night clothes, is sitting apart from the others. Old Maury, wearing a sheep-lined jacket, a hat, and bicycle clips at the bottom of his trousers, is standing motionless, ready to leave. Simon, lost in thought, is pacing up and down; alone he would have been wringing his hands. From beyond the wall, there is the sound of bustling, whispering, groans, sighs and words of encouragement.

MAURY: *(finally questioning the wall)* So? Do I or don't I go? Is it coming or not?

A VOICE: *(feminine and confident, answering with joyful energy)* Don't budge, it's not for tonight.

At that moment Lea appears, disheveled, and addresses Simon to explain.

LEA: False alarm.

Now Maury's daughter-in-law enters. She is a heavyset woman, still young, visibly robust and accustomed to work in the fields. She is holding some folded white sheets which she places on the back of a chair; then she removes the large basin which was on the table.

THE DAUGHTER-IN-LAW: She must rest.

MAURY: And what about the cramps?

THE DAUGHTER-IN-LAW: She did too much walking.

SIMON: *(approving)* There, I told her a million times, keep still, incubate, no, she's got to go racing around.

> *Maury, making himself at home as well he should, gets comfortable, takes some small glasses out of a closet and produces a bottle from one of the large pockets of his sheep-lined jacket. He fills up the glasses.*

LEA: *(protesting)* Not for me, Mr. Maury, nor my mother.

THE DAUGHTER-IN-LAW: *(to Simon)* Is this your first?

SIMON: No, no, I already have a nephew.

> *Maury laughs noisily.*

THE DAUGHTER-IN-LAW: *(grabbing one of the glasses)* What are you squealing for?

MAURY: Forget it, drink, drink! Here's to lovers. He's not the daddy, he's the uncle.

THE DAUGHTER-IN-LAW: You're always keeping everything hush-hush, right? If you'd let on, I'd've known.

SIMON: *(smiling foolishly and apologizing)* Uncle Simon.

MAURY: *(to his daughter-in-law)* I told you the little lady's husband is in Germany, like ours.

THE DAUGHTER-IN-LAW: I thought you were talking about Mrs. Lea's husband. *(To Lea)* Excuse me, Mrs. Lea.

LEA: No harm done.

MAURY: No, I told you the husband of...

He outlines a rounded belly.

THE DAUGHTER-IN-LAW: *(to Lea, interrupting Maury)* And Henri, whose is he? He's yours at least?

LEA: *(after glancing at Simon)* He's the son of one of my brothers.

SIMON: *(apologizing)* A sprawling brood.

THE DAUGHTER-IN-LAW: He's mighty cute, and also mighty polite.

LEA: Thank you.

THE DAUGHTER-IN-LAW: O.K., I'm getting myself home, she should stay in bed and get her pep back until it's ready to pop out. But no more walks or bicycling, all of that... *(She motions that it's over.)*

SIMON: *(approving)* Of course, of course.

LEA: *(to the daughter-in-law)* We ruined your night.

THE DAUGHTER-IN-LAW: Oh, for the amount of sleep we get... *(She yawns.)* Alone... Come on, Theodore, let's go home. *(To Maury)* Come along. What are you waiting for?

MAURY: *(without moving from the table)* Go on ahead.

THE DAUGHTER-IN-LAW: Let the people go to bed, you can suckle on that bottle tomorrow.

MAURY: Go on ahead, I tell you. We've got things to talk over. *(He drinks.)*

THE DAUGHTER-IN-LAW: *(exiting)* I'll leave you the basin and the sheets. *(She points to Maury.)* Just give him a good shove. When the bottle's empty, he'll be full.

Maury snickers.

LEA: *(walking the daughter-in-law back to the doorway)* Thank you for everything and good night—what's left of it.

She extends her hand awkwardly, but the daughter-in-law draws her close.

THE DAUGHTER-IN-LAW: *(kissing her on both cheeks)* And if there's any action on the front line, don't hesitate: knock, knock, knock... I'm like a hen, I sleep with one eye open...

The daughter-in-law exits. Lea bustles about with the sheets and the basin. She is holding back tears.

LEA: She's so nice...

MAURY: Sure, with other people, but at home...

He pours himself another small glass and one for Simon who now has two full glasses in front of him. Maury drinks. Simon stares at the two glasses. Lea also stares at them with a worried expression. Maury puts down his glass and waits. Simon looks first at Lea and then at Mrs. Schwartz who is dozing in her chair. Glancing back at Lea, he says:

SIMON: Leave us alone, we have things to talk over.

Lea goes over to Mrs. Schwartz and takes her by the arm to help her rise from the chair.

LEA: Mama...

THE MOTHER: *(immediately)* What time is it?

LEA: Almost two o'clock, time to go to sleep.

THE MOTHER: *(pushing her and turning away)* I just had my nap.

LEA: It's nighttime, mama. Bedtime, not naptime.

Mrs. Schwartz follows Lea docilely, but at the doorway to the next room she notices Maury and points to him.

THE MOTHER: What's he doing here?

LEA: Nothing, nothing. He's just come by to say hello.

THE MOTHER: *(still staring at Maury)* He's a bit deranged, no?

LEA: Of course not, what makes you say that?

THE MOTHER: *(still staring at him)* He looks it... Coming here like that, in the middle of the night... Isn't he O.K. at home? *(She follows Lea into the other room and asks:)* And Henrile?

LEA: *(while straightening out her bed)* Henri's asleep.

THE MOTHER: Where?

LEA: At Mr. Maury's daughter-in-law, in the village, down below.

THE MOTHER: What daughter-in-law? What village down below?

LEA: Come on, come on, stretch out your legs. I'll sit here at the edge of the bed for a while.

The mother suddenly re-enters, without her shawl, looking very dignified in her night clothes. She goes straight up to Maury and greets him warmly.

THE MOTHER: I'm delighted to meet you, Mr. Landlord...

Maury stands up, embarrassed and rather puzzled.

SIMON: *(murmuring)* She's saying hello.

MAURY: *(hastening to shake Mrs. Schwartz's hand as he grunts, embarrassed)* Hello, hello, Mrs. Girard, and good night, good night.

She walks away, very proper, and disappears again. She can be heard asking Lea:

THE MOTHER: Why's he always calling me Mrs. Girard? He's a bit deranged. *(Lea can be heard mumbling on the other side of the wall, Mrs. Schwartz laughs as Lea goes "sh!", "sh!". Finally, we hear Mrs. Schwartz's weary voice.)* What time is it, Lea?

Simon waits. Maury rotates the empty glass in his hands, preoccupied. After a long silence:

MAURY: O.K. here's the story. There's a boarding school in Ussel, in Corrèze, and I spoke to the father superior. It so happened, when my father-in-law was mayor of a small town there, he did him— I don't know—some favors. Anyway... Let's say this father superior —a good guy—owes my father-in-law, and so supposedly me, a good turn, since the old man is gone... O.K. They're not taking any new boarders, particularly it being the middle of term, but given the "special" circumstances... I stressed the kid is Alsatian and that his father's in detention out at Drancy. I said the right thing? His mother, too, no? *(Simon approves. Pause.)* So, if you still agree?

SIMON: *(after another pause)* Will he be O.K.?

MAURY: For studying? *(He looks up at the sky as a sign of ignorance, then explains.)* But he'll be kept in line, that's for sure. *(He pours himself another glassful.)*

SIMON: We can't keep letting him wrangle with every kid in the county, can we?

MAURY: *(drinks, then continues)* I have business around there, near Vignolles. Every two weeks, I'll check on how he's doing. And you, you can always drop him a line. You're not drinking?

SIMON: Yes I am. *(He empties one of the glasses and puts it down.)*

MAURY: The best cure-all... Headache? Drink up. Tooth stubs irking you? Drink up. Itchy corn on your foot? Quick, drink up. Contains thirty-three plants, personally picked, sorted, boiled and distilled by yours truly, from a secret family recipe, handed down from generation to generation, since, since...

SIMON: Vercingetorix?

MAURY: *(repeats approvingly)* Vercingetorix, absolutely, absolutely, Vercingetorix... *(He fills up his empty glass as he stands up.)* Fine, then... Monday, I'll take the kid. Write the name Maury on his school things. The father said it would be easier. I'll have new ration cards issued for him here at the town hall. As far as the expenses go, I said I could be held responsible... *(Simon nods. Maury drinks, then comments.)* One more for the road. Not that I'm going very far, but these days you've got to be pretty darn drunk just to walk straight. Go on, drink, it's homemade, I tell you. Chases away the blues. *(Simon obliges.)* Well, good, that's one more the Krauts won't get their hands on... You can have the rest... Use but don't abuse. Hail, hail to you.

> *He exits. As he goes, he can be heard whistling "Hail, hail to you, brave soldiers of the seventeenth..." Simon immediately begins to cough violently. Lea enters.*

SIMON: *(between two coughing fits)* Pour me some herbal tea. *(She obliges. Simon warms his hands on the bowl and looks up at Lea pitifully. She has settled down on the edge of the bed.)* So?

LEA: So?

> *In the ensuing silence, she dabs her eyes with a tiny silk handkerchief. Simon then pushes away his bowl and pours himself another glassful of the home-brewed elixir.*

SIMON: Help yourself, take a bed sheet, Lea. Don't try scooping up Niagara Falls with a teaspoon. Gets on my nerves.

Pause.

LEA: *(trying to seem detached)* What are we going to do?

SIMON: *(drinking)* About what? We've found a good little seminary for Henri, no? We just have to set your mother up in a Carmelite convent, Mauricette at the Children of Mary's—real fast—and us two, in a Swiss hospice for needy elderly...

LEA: And what if they make a priest out of him?

SIMON: Well, it's a noble profession, isn't it? Too seasonal, you think? *(Lea doesn't respond.)* It's better than being a rabbi, no? Especially for a Jew. No children to worry about, no mother-in-law, very little competition... Of course if you want to go into business for yourself, you're screwed...

Pause.

LEA: Monday is so soon. *(Simon doesn't respond.)* We could wait a bit, no? *(Simon doesn't respond.)* Just so he'd see the baby.

SIMON: It's better this way, Lea, much better... Plus a baby's a baby, no?

Silence.

LEA: *(finally whispers)* And what if something happens to Mauricette?

SIMON: *(after a pause, mastering himself)* Lea, this woman is the local expert on home deliveries. She knows! She knows!

LEA: *(whispering)* Is she going to do everything then?

SIMON: Of course not, the doctor will be here.

LEA: *(after a while)* Why wasn't he here tonight?

SIMON: *(after a while)* Because tonight wasn't the night, Lea! *(Pause.)* When the right night comes, old Maury will go fetch him, and he'll get here before the baby, I promise.

LEA: And the daughter-in-law's the one who decides when it's the right night?

SIMON: *(grunts)* Yes.

LEA: And what if that night their doctor happens to be busy?

SIMON: Lea, whose side are you on? I have the Krauts, the cops, Vichy, Laval, all on my back and you, you... What do you want from me, what do you want? *(Pause.)* Animals and people, that's the way they're all born around here. They're alive, aren't they? Yes or no?

> *Silence.*

LEA: *(pursuing her idea)* And what if we took her to the hospital?

SIMON: *(after a pause, mastering himself)* If the doctor says so, we'll do it. I'll tell Maury to keep his cattle truck ready, full of straw, just in case... O.K.?

> *Silence.*

48

LEA: *(finally, guardedly)* And what if it's a boy?

SIMON: *(sighs inadvertently while pretending not to understand)* Girl or boy, they come out the same, no?

LEA: *(insisting)* What if it's a boy Simon? What'll we do?

SIMON: *(after a pause)* I have a plan: we'll call him Marie-Thérèse, dress him in pink, and we won't clue anyone in! Later it'll be up to him to find his way.

Silence.

LEA: Simon, it means a lot to mother.

SIMON: Since mother, thank God, doesn't know the time of day anymore...

LEA: Don't worry, she still knows what distinguishes a Jewish boy!

SIMON: Advise her to forget. The time has come.

LEA: Mauricette is also worried sick. She confided in me.

SIMON: Where I come from, you worry before being knocked up, not after.

LEA: Simon, please.

SIMON: "Simon, please"... If you can't be careful, madam, you listen to the radio at night, or play rummy, not touchee-feelee... Or else you have the brains to get rid of it... You don't wait until you're knocked up and as big as a barrel to start worrying!

LEA: Simon, you're drunk!

SIMON: That's it, hear yee, hear yee, Simon's drunk! As soon as Charles got himself arrested I told her, "get rid of it!", no?

LEA: *(interrupting him)* Be quiet now, will you!

SIMON: Right, right. As usual the "be quiet now" policy. Always crying by night and smiling by day! Is this a good year, you think, for marketing new, oven-fresh baby Kikes, when we don't even know where to stash away the old ones and have to beg a priest in Corrèze so he'll deign take one on consignment?

LEA: Will you stop screaming, you're not alone.

SIMON: No kidding? No kidding! You're telling me? You're telling me? I know darn well I'm not alone, madam! They drive you crazy with their bullshit. "What'll we do if it's a boy, Simon?" And they moan and groan...

LEA: *(interrupting him)* No one's moaning and groaning! Some people here need their sleep, that's all.

SIMON: Some people! Some people! Damn it... I should sit outside, by the light of the moon—do you hear me? Plop my ass down in a puddle and keep yelling all day and all night to prevent you people from sleeping!

LEA: Outside, be my guest, yell as much as you want, but inside we're sleeping.

She slips into bed and turns her back to him. Pause.

SIMON: You all have no idea what it's like. *(Second pause.*

Lea doesn't react, she pretends to be sleeping. Simon continues.) You have no idea what it's like having an informer in your pants wherever you go, always being scared that any asshole in an officer's cap might pull your pants down and expose the undeniable, inalterable, naked proof of your absolute guilt... *(Another pause. Lea still pretends to be sleeping. Simon pours himself a glassful.)* Let's get it straight, ladies, if you can't strangle him at birth—which I can well understand—at least let him blend into the mass of innocent people, so we don't have to worry about leaving him on church steps, or in public toilets, and they can turn him into a full-fledged member of their dear Nation — make him a priest, a policeman, an executive, a delegate to the Board for Jewish Affairs, a beret manufacturer, anything! As long as it's useful to the community and he can escape this trap!

LEA: *(without turning)* No, if it's a boy, he'll be like his father, like you, like all the Jews on earth. I'll take care of it, I'll talk to the doctor. Go to sleep.

SIMON: Sleep! She'll take care of it! She'll talk to the doctor! Good grief, you're a real fanatic. And here I am trying to tell you that if I could stick it back on — with a thumbtack, even — I'd do it! Just to be free, free to come and go like everyone else in this damned country! So I'd have the right to just sit on my bench, in front of my house, on my street, boulevard Barbès!

LEA: Simon, for once Charles and Mauricette are right, not you. Now, please be nice and stop talking, I'm sleepy.

SIMON: *(bringing his hand up to his head)* Excuse me, but I don't follow you anymore. Who's right and who's wrong? You say I'm usually right—and I'm very grateful you're finally admitting it— but, you say, this time, they're right!

O.K., right about what? I've had a lot to drink, I'm no longer in complete command of my stupendous faculties, if you could please elaborate, or give me a little hint...

LEA: *(turning toward him and whispering)* Now's the time to bring Jewish children into the world, Simon. Now.

SIMON: *(whispers after a pause)* Why?

LEA: *(turning away after a pause)* I don't know why, I just feel it in my heart.

SIMON: Unbelievable, unbelievable. She doesn't know why, she feels it in her heart. Miracle on the Plateau of a Thousand Cows: Lea Zilberberg, born Schwartz, parts with her endemic atheism, tinged with empirical communism, and rediscovers her ancestors' faith and the meaning of the covenant! Hallelujah, hallelujah! She is chosen for life. O.K., O.K., let's assume children are necessary to perpetuate this mess, O.K.... But why would you need Jewish children? Since no one wants them around anymore? Why insist? It's bad form to keep imposing and it's unhealthy. Me, now, I can't even see the letter "J" printed in a newspaper without getting palpitations. I see June, I read Jew, I see kite, I read Kike. What kind of disease is that, Lea, who'll cure me, who? And why? Why're they sticking "Jew" everywhere, everywhere — on our I.D.s, on our chests... Why's it the only thing they talk about — on the radio, in the newspapers? What's it all about? What does it all mean? Soon you'll see, even the local hens will check before laying their eggs. "Cluck, cluck, cluck, is this eggie for a Kike, is this eggie for a Kike?" And rotten eggs will plop out, with "Jew" engraved in gothic lettering on the shells—eggs with no white and no yolk—crummy, square eggs that won't fit into any egg cups, and that the wailing yokels will sell us for a king's ransom!

LEA: *(curling up to sleep)* I'll tune in for the rest tomorrow. Good n-i-i-i-ght!

SIMON: Good n-i-i-i-ght, ha! *(Pause.)* And what does that mean, "I'll talk to the doctor"? Do you even know him? Do you? *(Silence. Lea no longer reacts. After drinking straight from the bottle and emptying it, Simon slips into bed.)* In any case, you're right, there's no point in getting worked up about this faucet problem, there's a fifty percent chance we'll be spared any kind of plumbing. The odds are reasonable, no? Let's just hope!

LEA: *(after a pause, without turning)* She said it would be a boy.

SIMON: Who did? Your mother?

LEA: No, your daughter-in-law.

SIMON: My daughter-in-law?

LEA: Maury's daughter-in-law...

SIMON: What the hell does she know? What the hell?

LEA: When you carry it all in front, she says, like a balloon, it's a boy...

SIMON: In front, in back, I've got a fifty-fifty chance, fifty-fifty! And don't anybody try to gyp me on this one. I'm sick and tired, really sick and tired. Fifty-fifty, that's it, or else count me out. *(He turns off the light and groans.)* I think herbal tea makes me jumpy, Lea. I feel so tense, so tense. I can see I'll have trouble falling asleep again. *(He sighs. Silence settles in for a moment. They both try to sleep. Then, beyond the wall, Mrs. Schwartz can be heard humming the lullaby. Simon sits up immediately.)* No, goddamnit, no. She's going to wake Mauricette! Do something, Lea, do something!

MAURICETTE: *(from beyond the wall)* I'm not sleeping, Simon, I'm not sleeping.

LEA: *(worried)* What's wrong, darling? Aren't you well?

MAURICETTE: I'm incubating. *(Pause.)* I can feel them moving.

SIMON: *(to Lea, horrified)* What's she saying? What's she saying?

MAURICETTE: Twins, Simon, twins, I hope!

> *Darkness falls. The lullaby gets louder and reaches a climax. It is interrupted by the first cry of a new-born baby. Sudden blackout and silence.*

SCENE 5

An infant's burps and cries can be heard in the dark, accompanied by the sinister ring of an alarm clock. Simon tosses and turns in bed, then sitting on the edge, talks in a low voice.

SIMON: She takes after you, Lea. No sooner born and already she doesn't know why, but she senses she should cry at night. *(Beyond the wall, they are quietly getting up, picking up the baby and calming her. Simon listens.)* A little warm milkie-milk. Rockabye baby on the treetop... *(He rises and begins dressing hurriedly.)*

LEA: What are you doing?

SIMON: *(hurrying)* I'm freezing. *(He goes up to the window and opens the shutter. Early morning lights up the room.)* It's almost time.

> *We see a clothesline stretched across the room with diapers hanging to dry. Piles of laundry are stacked on the table. Some clothes lie folded by a knapsack. Simon walks behind the clothesline, pokes around the stove, then goes to wash his face over the sink. The diapers partially hide him from Lea who stays in bed momentarily, silently watching him, and then gets up.*

SIMON: What are you doing?

LEA: Making herbal tea.

SIMON: Don't bother. Old Maury's going to show up.

LEA: *(while putting up the water)* I'm not going to let you go without something warm in your stomach. *(Simon is washing himself. Lea pushes the laundry aside, sets two bowls down on the table, and asks:)* Simon, do you think you're doing the right thing?

SIMON: I don't know. *(Pause.)* This is my first war, Lea, both as uncle and scapegoat. *(Mechanically, she packs some clothes and personal effects in the little knapsack and places the rest in a suitcase. He continues.)* I'm responsible for him, no? No?

LEA: *(finally)* You told me that over there he'd be kept in line, at least.

SIMON: He left during a game of hide and seek. And boarding school—even a Catholic boarding school—isn't a jail, is it?

LEA: What about waiting a bit longer?

SIMON: *(glancing at her)* Waiting for what? What are you doing?

LEA: Packing your things.

SIMON: Don't, I'll do it.

She continues.

LEA: What about putting out a search notice?

SIMON: Under what name? Henri Girard Maury Schwartz Zilberberg? Don't stuff in all the shirts that have frayed collars!

LEA: There aren't any others.

SIMON: O.K., O.K., then go ahead, stuff, stuff.

LEA: We could register with the authorities here and...

SIMON: *(interrupting her, he suddenly appears between the diapers, his face covered with shaving cream and holding a razor.)* Register with the authorities? What authorities? The cops have joined the crooks, Lea. They don't allow you to work, or move, they rob you with impunity—and this in the name of the law, Lea, in the name of the law!... Marshal bla-bla-bla donates his person to the Goys and the statutes on Jews to the Kikes... And every god-given day, experts on the Jewish Question rack their brains to knock you down even further... I won't ever be registered again, Lea, never again. *(He disappears momentarily then reappears brandishing his razor.)* If we pull through, one day they'll have to register with us. They'll have to register, not us! *(He disappears and yells almost immediately.)* Shit! Goddamnit! Hand me a diaper, I cut myself. Register! *(He wipes his face with the diaper then throws it aside.)* The other kid's father also wanted to go by the rule book—lodge a formal complaint, on principle, he said...

LEA: Did he take a lot of money from him?

SIMON: Of course not! But he also swiped his ration card and his Boy Scouts of France booklet. His name now is Mathieu Lerrand, he's born in Tulle, sixteen years old.

LEA: Sixteen? Henrile?

SIMON: You thick or something? That's what's on the papers he pinched. Fortunately the father superior was able to talk Lerrand senior out of it and warn old Maury who compensated him. There you have it. And we've been waiting ever since and I'm fed up waiting, really fed up, Lea. Do you understand?

Silence.

LEA: *(in a low voice)* And what if he got picked up crossing the line?

SIMON: They don't pick up kids, Lea. Everyone can see he's a kid, and not sixteen. No, no, he's up there, and, you'll see, I'll grab him by the nape of the neck and drag him back.

LEA: Simon, don't be too hard on him.

SIMON: "Don't be too hard on him"... This kid has been weighing on me for months, Lea, like a piece of lead, right here, on the back of my neck. "Don't be too hard on him!"... Am I responsible for him, yes or no? Yes or no?... *(The baby in the next room starts crying again. Simon buries his head in the diaper he's been using as a towel and mutters.)* Dear God, what have I done to be tormented like this by other people's children? What have I done?

> *Mauricette enters wheeling a baby carriage; inside a child is crying and wiggling about. She wheels the baby up and down, calmly and attentively, quieting her with her voice.*

LEA: *(pouring Simon some herbal tea)* Drink, drink while it's hot.

> *Simon finishes dressing, then slips on the heavy city overcoat Henri had been covered with in the first scene. He puts on a felt hat with a turned down rim, stands in front of Mauricette and Lea and asks:*

SIMON: How do I look?

LEA: *(without conviction)* Good.

MAURICETTE: The only things missing are gloves and a cane and you'd be Mr. Elegant.

LEA: Mr. Elephant if you had a trunk. *(She sighs.)* You'll go see everybody up there?

SIMON: I'll see them all. Do I look normal?

MAURICETTE: Yes, normal.

SIMON: No, Goy! Do I look like a Goy?

LEA: You have Maury's fake papers?

SIMON: *(automatically tapping his breast pocket to check)* Yes, yes. *(He turns around where he's standing.)* So, you think I look O.K.? There isn't even a mirror around here. *(A whistle call is heard outside.)* Maury!... *(He kisses Mauricette and slips on the little knapsack with Lea's help and asks:)* Did you pack everything? *(She nods. He embraces her. Simon mumbles:)* We'll remember this life, eh Lea, we'll remember it... when we're in Bagneux, six feet under, in the tomb of the Future Brotherhood of the Sons and Daughters of Galicia...

LEA: Stop by Mimé Reizl's and Uncle Isy's too...

A louder whistle call is heard from outside.

SIMON: *(answering everyone simultaneously)* Yes, yes...

MAURICETTE: Try and find out about Charles and the others...

SIMON: *(from the door)* I'll grab Henri by the ear and drag him all the way back here. There, that's all...

LEA: Go, go. *(She kisses him again. He runs out, then runs back in and thrusts his head inside the baby carriage for a second. The child immediately begins to cry.)* Simon!

SIMON: *(he pops his head back out and says bitterly:)* So much for that!

> *Then he rushes back toward the door, stops and searches his pockets hurriedly.*

LEA: What's missing?

SIMON: I don't have a handkerchief.

LEA: *(handing him a diaper)* Here.

SIMON: You think big. That's good, thank you.

> *He dries his eyes, stuffs the diaper in his pocket and exits. Outside he hails Maury while Mauricette yells after him:*

MAURICETTE: Have a coffee at the corner of Labat street, next to the Barbès Galleries' wooden man, and think of me!...

> *Lea shuts the door again. Silence sets in for a moment.*

LEA: *(noting in disappointment)* He didn't even drink his herbal tea.

Mauricette walks the baby carriage back and forth to calm the child. Maury and Simon suddenly burst into the room again.

MAURY: *(yelling)* Who the hell stuck me with this city slicker? *(To Lea)* You sending him off to a ball or something? Go ahead, take it off... Wear sheep's clothing and the wolves will devour you... Come on, come on...

> *He helps him remove the knapsack and the coat. He rips off his own sheep-lined jacket and hands it to Simon who protests.*

SIMON: I'm going to Paris, not out to make hay.

MAURY: Once a peasant always a peasant, even in Paris. Put this on please, put it on! Please! *(Simon complies. Maury rips off Simon's hat and replaces it with his own beret.)* O.K., that's more like it. A regular local, a regular Maury from Château-Ponsac. Otherwise why'd I bother digging up the peasant ancestry recorded in your family booklet?

SIMON: *(worried, questioning Lea and Mauricette)* How do I look?

MAURY: Hurry, hurry. The bus is leaving. We'll have to cut through the fields now. *(Maury puts on Simon's black coat and hat. He turns ceremoniously toward the ladies, affecting an urban bearing.)* Ladies, miss, the morning's best regards. O.K., we're off.

SIMON: *(removing a small bottle out of the pocket of the fur jacket)* Here, this is yours.

MAURY: Thank you. *(He rifles through the coat pockets and*

removes a diaper.) And this is yours?

SIMON: *(embarrassed)* Thank you.

> *Maury shoves Simon out the door.*

LEA: *(yelling from the doorstep)* You didn't have anything hot to drink! *(They can be seen hurrying away, struggling up the embankment.)* They didn't have anything hot!

MAURICETTE: Maury must have had his wine and bouillon brew.

> *Silence. Lea shuts the door again, goes to the table, sits down and drinks her herbal tea. Finally she raises her eyes and looks at Mauricette.*

LEA: Would you like some? *(Mauricette nods. Lea serves her, then explains.)* Crossing the fields, his feet will get soaked.

> *Mrs. Schwartz appears at the bedroom door.*

THE MOTHER: Simon gone?

LEA: Yes, he said to say good-bye to you.

THE MOTHER: He said nothing at all. He forgot me...

LEA: He told me to tell you. He was afraid of waking you up.

> *Silence. Lea serves her some herbal tea.*

THE MOTHER: He goes off and leaves you all alone?

MAURICETTE: Mama, please...

LEA: He'll be back, he'll be back. He won't be away for long.

THE MOTHER: *(drinking)* Wish I could go away and stay away.

MAURICETTE: Mama...

THE MOTHER: What am I doing here again, huh?

MAURICETTE: You're hiding, like everyone else.

THE MOTHER: Hiding? In deference to what? Your father would never have let me hide like this... *(The child suddenly starts crying again while, behind the row of diapers, Mauricette is bustling about near the stove; she mumbles a few words, trying to calm her. The roosters cock-a-doodle-doo outside. The child cries even louder.)* Serenade time. My daughters never cried, never. My son, yes. Boys cry more than girls, at first. And Henrile? Henrile's my son's son, isn't he?

LEA: *(nodding wearily)* Yes, mama, yes.

THE MOTHER: So why doesn't he ever come and see me? Grandsons are supposed to come and see their grandparents, aren't they?

LEA: Yes, mama. Mama...

THE MOTHER: Eh?

LEA: If you could try and remember not to speak Yiddish anymore.

THE MOTHER: *(after staring at her a moment)* Now that your

madman is gone, Lea dear, what are you afraid of, what are you afraid of?

LEA: When there are people around, mama, you must not speak Yiddish anymore. Never, you understand? Never in front of people. When we're alone like this, O.K., but remember, not in front of people. Understand?

THE MOTHER: People? What people?

LEA: People, mama, people.

THE MOTHER: *(after a pause)* Back home too, in Poland, we used to go to the country to get eggs, butter, what have you... but only for a day or two, never more, never. The country there was awful, Lea, awful, like here.

LEA: Mama, get dressed, you'll catch a cold.

THE MOTHER: I wish a cold would catch me... There isn't even a café, a store, or a sidewalk around here. If misfortune could spirit me away and spare the others, it wouldn't be a misfortune. No, it would be... *(She turns to Lea.)* You're crying?

LEA: *(wiping her eyes)* No, I'm in stitches.

THE MOTHER: Why're you crying, silly, tell me?

LEA : *(after a pause)* I miss the madman, mama. I really feel like yelling right now and there's no one to yell at... I never should've let him go. And I shouldn't have let Henri go to the priests... I shouldn't have... *(She buries her face in her hands.)*

THE MOTHER: *(after some thought)* It was before?

LEA: Before what, mama?

THE MOTHER: *(still deep in thought, repeating)* Before?

LEA: Yes, mama, it was before.

> *Mrs. Schwartz suddenly becomes very active.*

THE MOTHER: What time is it?

MAURICETTE: *(muttering as she walks by with the baby carriage)* Seven.

THE MOTHER: *(surprised)* Already? Oh yes, that's life, time goes by, you stay alone, the day is over, you get bored, the others leave, and you stay.

MAURICETTE: Seven in the morning, mama, seven in the morning!

THE MOTHER: Do you think I'm deaf too? *(She stands up.)* "Seven in the morning"... Is that a reason to yell at your mother? *(She goes to the adjoining room and can be heard mumbling as she goes back to bed.)* "Seven in the morning"!

> *Lea is seated at the table. Mauricette is next to her, rocking the child who is peacefully sleeping in the carriage. Time seems to have stopped. Then blackout.*

SCENE 6

Broad daylight. The room is in disarray, but the diapers have disappeared. Lea is sewing. She is sitting next to the table, facing the door. Mauricette, her back turned, is using the sewing machine. It is portable, sits on a piece of furniture, has a handle and is at least a half a century old. Mrs. Schwartz is walking around in the adjoining room. She might be rocking the child in the carriage. During the scene she might make a brief appearance at the doorway. Mr. Apfelbaum enters by the half-open door; he is wearing city clothes, including a hat and an umbrella. Only his empty black canvas bag, muddy galoshes and black hands betray him. He seems out of breath and rather distraught. Lea, absorbed in her work, glances briefly in his direction. The rest of the time she remains engrossed in her sewing, hardly listening to Apfelbaum's chaotic soliloquy. Mauricette remains with her back turned, absorbed in work. On the table, a jumble of manufactured shirts suggests the two sisters' activity. There is an ambiance of work and complicity. An iron might be warming on the stove; Lea and Mauricette might do some ironing. Mrs. Schwartz might come and inspect her daughters' handiwork at the end of the scene.

APFELBAUM: *(entering)* Hello, Mrs. Lea!

LEA: Hello.

APFELBAUM: *(in the direction of Mauricette's back)* Madam.

LEA: *(to Mauricette)* It's Mr. Apfelbaum.

MAURICETTE: *(sewing uninterruptedly)* Hello, hello...

Silence, except for the brief squeaking of Mauricette's machine.

APFELBAUM: *(to Lea)* You know what? *(Silence. Apfelbaum finally nods as though Lea had guessed.)* They want to de-naturalize us. Really, really. It's the deputy mayor...the brother of the coalman for whom I ... *(He gestures with his blackened hands as though he were sawing wood.)* "And what will that make us, your honor, when they de-naturalize us?" I asked casually while cutting the wood. "Whatever you were before." "Before? Bessarabian, Moldavian, Rumanian, Russian, Serbo-Croatian, Moldo-Walachian, what do I know? "You mean you don't know what you were before?" "Sir, over there, in the Carpathians, I would have given an arm and a leg to become French, but as for finding out what I was, I couldn't have cared less. Besides it kept changing all the time." *(Silence.)* What do they know, what do they know about life? *(Pause.)* "You should go to Nice, to the Italian zone, you'd be better off, "he says, "the Italians protect Jews." "And who protects the Italians? Who?" *(Pause during which he rubs his solar plexus while taking a deep breath.)* And apart from that? Any news?

LEA: No, just this card from the occupied zone where he says he's still investigating and has high hopes.

Apfelbaum nods silently, then sits at the edge of Mrs. Schwartz's straw-bottomed armchair and mumbles.

APFELBAUM: May I? *(Lea nods. Pause.)* They're eliminating the free zone but they're keeping the demarcation line. What do you think that means?

LEA: *(shrugging)* That's the way it is.

APFELBAUM: *(approving)* That's the way it is, exactly, that's the way it is, for everything! *(He sighs.)* You know, I think they're treating us badly, very badly. What are they after? What more do they want from us? They want us to work? Have we ever refused? Sixteen, seventeen, eighteen hours a day, by candlelight during strikes, on Saturdays, Sundays, holidays—am I right? When the interim administrative manager aryanizer marched into my place—may he suffocate in my rags—he asked to be taken directly to the premises. "The premises", I said, "these are the premises, sir! "This is it, sir, my main place of business, outlets and all, right here!" So then he asked to see my employees. I said, "My wife cooks, my son is still in school." So then he asks to see my cashbooks, balance sheet, stock inventory, files, suppliers, clients. I had prepared it all on a single sheet of paper. I said, "Here! Everything's listed. On one side of the sheet the people from whom I buy the scraps and remnants, on the other, the names and addresses of the people to whom I resell." So he starts yelling, what kind of bookkeeping is this? What kind of balance sheet or inventory? It's an outrage, and I'm nothing but a ragman. "Me, a ragman, sir?" Or else I'm hiding something, and if that's the case I won't get away with it, he'll call the cops. "The cops? Fine, call them!" "Your stock, where's your stock?" "It's all here, sir!" "Your profits, where are your profits?" "Here!" *(He taps his belly.)* "Here! We earn enough to fill our stomachs, once a week we go to the movies, or the Yiddish theater on Lancry street. Down in the courtyard, there's the handcart I use for work, in the kitchen there's a plate-warmer with two burners, a sink, and soon—God willing but it's unlikely—a shower in the toilet. So much for my bookkeeping, sir, that's the extent of my balance sheet!" He yelled and yelled his head off. "France needs textiles, textile businesses must keep operating!" "Who with?" I asked, "Who with?" Then he calmed down, and I gave him a detailed explanation of how the textile business really works. He was a complete ignoramus... Then next thing you know, boom, he's catapulted into the position of supervisor, manager, organizer, aryanizer... O.K., I signed and left him the keys. Liquidated! That's it! You stay there day and night, you sort the scraps, you measure the fabric remnants and lug two-hundred-pound bundles up those winding stairs. *(He groans.)* What's going to happen to my Daniel if they denaturalize us, his mother and me? Everything's always been so complicated for him, everything, even finding the right size cap. *(Silence. Suddenly Apfelbaum stands up decisively.)* O.K., here I am talking and talking, and meanwhile I'm not getting food supplies. It's getting harder and harder, isn't it? The cost of living, as they say, keeps going up. Only the cost of our lives keeps going down, right? *(He laughs.)* Last week I went into the hills, near Lubac, even further, to a small, isolated village. The first house I come to I ask if they have anything edible for sale. "We've got nothing left." I keep asking. "Anything— chestnuts, rutabagas, Jerusalem artichokes..." "Nothing." Then he adds, "Ever since there are Jews in these parts we're wiped out. Nothing's left for us. They buy everything. People deprive themselves to sell to them. They're driving the prices up too high, you understand?" Then he says President Laval even said so on the radio, "It's the Jews who are teaching our French peasants to steal." Yes, yes, the Jews! Then he tells me to come in for a drink. What could I do? I go in, have a drink. Then he tells me he has tobacco, Jerusalem artichokes, but the prices! All because of the Jews... He's even ashamed to quote them. Then he tells me he has dry sausage and lard. So I said to him, "You're not going to charge me what you charge the Jews, are you?" "No, no." *(Pause.)* What are you working on, Mrs. Lea?

LEA: Shirts.

APFELBAUM: Shirts? Wonderful! But where did you get the material?

LEA: From old sheets.

APFELBAUM: Old sheets? Wonderful! Wonderful!

LEA: First I soak them in walnut stain.

APFELBAUM: Walnut stain!

LEA: To dye them a bit.

APFELBAUM: Wonderful! Wonderful! *(He fondles a shirt on the table, then says)* You know, Mrs. Lea, what I like best about us isn't our history, our rabbis, our laws, it isn't our thinkers, our writers, our geniuses—no, it's this: the sheets, Mrs. Lea, the sheets and the walnut stain. It's what they envy us for, Mrs. Lea, this... *(Overcome with emotion, he presses the shirt against his heart; Mauricette and Lea exchange a glance. Mr. Maury appears, a basket on his arm. Apfelbaum hastily puts the shirt on the table, grabs his hat, canvas bag and umbrella, and shouts.)* Mrs. Lea, Mrs. Mauricette, Mrs. Schwartz, good evening! *(Then in a low voice)* Kiss the baby for me and keep me informed, eh, keep me informed!

He is at the door.

LEA: Say hello to the missis and to Daniel.

APFELBAUM: Will do, will do. *(On his way out he greets Maury ceremoniously.)* Sir...

Maury responds by mumbling "sir" indistinctly while watching him exit. Apfelbaum disappears. Silence.

MAURY: *(to Lea, sternly)* Mr. Simon wouldn't approve.

LEA: *(curtly)* Of what?

MAURY: *(pointing to the door)* Of seeing him hang around here. *(Lea shrugs her shoulders. New silence. Everyone is absorbed in their work. Maury speaks while emptying the contents of his basket on the table.)* Should learn to keep the door shut. *(Lea sews, Mauricette runs the sewing machine, Maury finishes emptying the basket and announces:)* The butcher in Malmores would like one.

MAURICETTE: How big is he?

MAURY: He's taller than me.

LEA: His neck size, we have to have his neck size.

Maury nods. Mrs. Schwartz enters and sits down at the table. She fondles the shirts and the vegetables with delight. Blackout.

SCENE 7

Daylight. Mrs. Schwartz and Maury are seated at the table facing each other. They are supposed to be playing a game of dominoes. Lea is seated next to her mother, peeling vegetables. Mauricette and the child are absent. Next to the sewing machine there is a pile of unfinished shirts. Deep silence reigns. Maury waits, concentrating intensely. Mrs. Schwartz yawns conspicuously.

MAURY: *(to Lea, after a pause)* It's your mother's turn.

LEA: *(to her mother)* It's your turn.

Mrs. Schwartz nods like someone who knows but feels unconcerned. Suddenly she picks up one of the domino pieces and places it at the edge of the board. Then she stares at Maury with a look of satisfaction. Maury looks at the board in astonishment, glances at Mrs. Schwartz, and murmurs to Lea:

MAURY: What's she doing? *(Lea takes a look. Maury gets worked up.)* Should be a blank or a six and she puts down a double four.

LEA: *(pushing away the double four with the tip of her knife)* Mama, you need a blank or a six.

THE MOTHER: *(peremptorily)* And what if I don't have them? *(She puts the double four back down, this time at the other edge of the board.)* Don't worry, I know how to play, I know how to play. It's important that I get rid of this one real fast. It's a big one. Be quiet!

Maury fidgets and grumbles, then asks:

MAURY: What's she saying?

LEA: *(taking the double four and giving it back while glancing at the other pieces which her mother tries to hide from her)* She has no blanks or sixes.

MAURY: *(majestic)* Of course not. *(He is triumphant, exultant.)* She has to draw another piece.

LEA: Mama, dig in.

THE MOTHER: What? Are you siding with that embezzler against your own mother?

LEA: You have to draw pieces until you get a good one.

THE MOTHER: Fat chance. Let him draw pieces, if that's what he enjoys! Or let him get his daughter-in-law to do it.

LEA: Mama, you're the one who has no blanks or sixes and it's your turn.

THE MOTHER: He's doing it on purpose, deliberately cornering me.

LEA: Mama, that's the game.

MAURY: *(worried)* What's she saying?

LEA: *(hesitates, then affirms)* She'd rather you drew for her.

MAURY: What? I can't do that! I'll find out what she has!

LEA: *(annoyed)* Mama, draw one already!

THE MOTHER: No! He purposely hoarded all the blanks

and sixes, now he wants me to draw what's left over. Go see what he's got. Go on.

LEA: Mama...

THE MOTHER: I'm not playing anymore. Let him go outside and play with his cows. He smells, doesn't he? He smells of cows.

LEA: *(losing her temper)* He doesn't own any cows, mama. Stop it, mama, will you?

MAURY: What's she saying?

LEA: She's a bit tired.

MAURY: *(worried)* Is she quitting?

LEA: *(to her mother)* Are you quitting?

> *Defiant, the mother doesn't answer. She starts peeling vegetables.*

MAURY: *(bewildered, after a pause)* Well. O.K., then, I'll make an exception in this particular instance, I'll, I'll draw one for her, there... I'm drawing one for you Mrs. Girard! *(He draws a piece and after examining it, delicately adds it to Mrs. Schwartz's pile with a little smile.)* Ah? No...

> *Mrs. Schwartz looks away.*

LEA: *(to her mother)* Don't make the peelings so thick, mama.

> *Mrs. Schwartz puts down the Jerusalem artichoke.*

MAURY: *(withdrawing another piece from the container)* Really, Mrs. Girard, this isn't your lucky day.

THE MOTHER: Girard this, Girard that, this man's got his head screwed on backwards, Lea. Ask him if he thinks he's Napoleon.

Maury looks questioningly at Lea.

MAURY: What?

Lea keeps peeling without responding.

THE MOTHER: *(while Maury picks another piece)* Tell him they recently changed the rules in Paris. Now it's the person with the most pieces who wins.

Lea sighs wearily, repressing the urge to laugh.

LEA: Mama...

Maury draws another piece and pretends to be surprised and sorry.

MAURY: No? Again? Mrs. Girard...

Maury's grandchild runs in at this point, out of breath and panic-stricken. He begins yelling at the entrance.

THE CHILD: Grandpa! Grandpa! *(Then he whispers.)* Mom sent me to tell you the police are down below, and they're coming up here to take our Jews away!

MAURY: *(standing up)* What are you saying?

THE CHILD: I ran, grandpa. I ran! As soon as mom told me to come up here, I ran. They searched the house, they asked her a whole lot of questions.

MAURY: Oh, holy shit! Filthy crap! Better decamp, come on, quick, let's go!

LEA: But where? Where can we go?

MAURY: I'll put you up in the chapel for the night, up above, at the Gros-Bois pass. Come on, come on, let's go, let's go!

Lea, panicked, hastily fills up a bag and a basket.

LEA: What about Mauricette? And the baby?

MAURY: *(while ripping off the blankets)* I'll take care of them, don't worry... Just get your mother out of here.

THE MOTHER: *(watching them)* Why's he undoing the beds? Undoing beds in the middle of the day brings bad luck. What's going on now, is he a bad loser?

LEA: Mama, put on your other shoes.

MAURY: *(to the child)* Take them straight up to the top.

LEA: I know where it is, I know where it is.

MAURY: *(to the child)* You'll find the key under the flat stone, where I showed you, remember?

THE CHILD: Yes, grandpa, I know.

MAURY: *(at the doorstep, scrutinizing the road in the distance)* It's the Wars of Religion, the Wars of Religion all over again! Hurry, ladies, hurry, please!

LEA: *(to her mother)* Your shoes.

THE MOTHER: These are the only ones I'm comfortable in.

LEA: You need heavy shoes, mama, for walking.

THE MOTHER: I refuse to put on those galoshes, Lea, no matter what.

LEA: *(pulling off her mother's high-heeled shoes and replacing them with the coarse, laced booties)* Mama, you're putting these on and that's that.

THE MOTHER: *(docilely allowing her to lace them up)* Where are we going now?

MAURY: Stop dawdling, for God's sake, come on!

> *The child takes Mrs. Schwartz's hand and leads her toward the door.*

THE CHILD: Come on, little grandma, come on.

> *They exit. Lea picks up the blankets, grabs her bag and exits. The room remains empty. Maury can be heard offstage.*

MAURY: I'll help you cross the embankment. When you get to the woods you can take your time. You'll be under cover. *(Silence. The stage remains empty. The wind slams the door back and forth. Maury re-enters, irate; he marches up and down momentarily, then explodes.)* Take away my Jews, the nerve! *(Finally he stares at the board, examines it carefully, picks up Mrs. Schwartz's pieces and the ones remaining in the container. Then he sits down at Mrs. Schwartz's place and becomes engrossed in the game. A knock at the door. Maury doesn't move.)* Come on in, it's open.

Policeman #1 enters.

POLICEMAN #1: Girard family?

MAURY: Gérard? Who's that? There are no Gérards here. That's a good one, you don't even know whose place you've come to anymore? Maury! Maury!

POLICEMAN #1: *(raising a hand to his visor)* Hello, Mr. Maury. Say, it's still quite a climb to your place, eh?

MAURY: And so why'd you bother?

POLICEMAN #1: My colleagues and me we're required.

MAURY: Required? By whom?

POLICEMAN #1: *(after a pause during which he glances around at the disorderliness)* We're rounding up all illegal foreigners residing on county territory.

MAURY: And here is where you're hoping to round up foreigners?

POLICEMAN #1: *(after a pause)* We've got our reasons, maybe.

MAURY: *(unflustered)* What are they?

POLICEMAN #1: *(lowering his voice)* Letters and things like that. *(Silence.)* We stopped by your house down below. We saw your daughter-in-law. Did your grandson tell you?

MAURY: My grandson? Haven't seen him.

Silence.

POLICEMAN #2: *(pushing the door open and entering with a heavy tread)* There's no one in the surrounding area. Hello.

POLICEMAN #1: *(to Maury, pointing to the other room)* May I?

MAURY: By all means. *(Policeman #1 crosses the room and disappears into the other room. Maury quizzes him.)* And what do you do with your illegal foreigners, if I may ask?

POLICEMAN #1: *(off)* We send them to Nexon.

MAURY: Nexon?

POLICEMAN #2: *(clarifying)* Nexon, Haute-Vienne.

MAURY: And what's Nexon, Haute-Vienne?

POLICEMAN #2: A camp.

MAURY: Oh, really, you don't say, in Haute-Vienne.

POLICEMAN #2: *(nodding)* Yes, here in Corrèze there aren't any.

MAURY: Nexon...

POLICEMAN #2: *(continuing)* Then in Nexon their status is

legalized, if needed.

POLICEMAN #1: *(re-entering)* O.K., well, after checking the premises, we're able to certify there's no one here. Right?

Policeman #2 agrees, swaying back and forth.

MAURY: You want to see my I.D. papers? So you won't have trekked up here for nothing!

POLICEMAN # 1: Come now... come now...

MAURY: Then, how about one for the road?

He takes a small bottle out of his breast pocket and sets it down on the table.

POLICEMAN # 1: No, no, we still have a long way to go.

MAURY: That's just it.

POLICEMAN #2: *(intrigued by the game of dominoes)* What's that?

MAURY: Dominoes.

POLICEMAN #2: You play dominoes?

MAURY: To kill time while I heat up the soup...

POLICEMAN #2: Alone?

MAURY: When you're old... You want to play a game?

POLICEMAN #2: Not while I'm on the job.

MAURY: Come back whenever you like.

POLICEMAN #2: Well, I'm not saying I won't.

MAURY: I warn you, I'm a scientific player.

POLICEMAN #2: Scientific? Good God! In that case, I'll send you my kid.

> *All three laugh, raise their glasses, drink, and click their tongues in appreciation. Maury is proud. Policeman #1 sits down, puts his cap down on a nearby chair, and talks while taking out a black notebook and a pencil.*

POLICEMAN #1: O.K., I reckon we can certify in writing that no one by the name of Girard or Gérard lives in these quarters. Right?

> *Policeman #2 nods gravely, then collapses into a chair suddenly, declaring:*

POLICEMAN #2: I've had it.

MAURY: *(looking at the policeman)* Really, it's a heck of a job they've got you doing...

POLICEMAN #2: *(pulling himself together)* Hell, respect for the law must be enforced, or else...

MAURY: As far as I'm concerned, under my roof, there's only one law! To your health!

> *He raises his glass inviting the policemen to raise theirs, then all three clink glasses. The three men drink.*

POLICEMAN #1: *(still sitting)* Your daughter-in-law helped my wife for my first-born. A nice young woman. Your daughter-in-law, I mean; so's my wife, huh, so's my wife. *(He laughs, embarrassed, then stands up suddenly.)* O.K., come on, there's more ahead, onwards, one-two, one-two, march.

MAURY: How about another drop? *(The policemen protest vigorously, covering their glasses with their hands, then they give in. Maury serves them.)* And supposing I come across illegal foreigners, what should I say to them?

POLICEMAN #1: That's up to you. We ...

POLICEMAN #2: *(half-heartedly)* You're supposed to report them to us, yes.

POLICEMAN #1: *(pursuing his idea)* As far as we're concerned, we checked out the premises as required by law and saw for ourselves you weren't sheltering anyone, neither down below, nor up here. As for the rest... *(He gestures with his hand.)*

POLICEMAN #2: *(at the doorstep)* However, for your information, you ought to know that if we'd found you were sheltering illegal foreigners—or anyone else, in fact, whose status is illegal or in violation of the Labor Service, et cetera—you'd have been charged with a statutory offense, and you wouldn't have been sent to Nexon, but straight to Limoges.

MAURY: You don't say!

POLICEMAN #2: That's the way it is, my friend, you might as well know. So long.

He clicks his heels half-heartedly. At that moment Simon appears at the entrance and stops short, stunned to see the policemen.

MAURY: *(instantly)* Well, well, come on in, silly goose, you all alone this time? *(Simon nods. Maury kisses him on both cheeks, then drags him inside and introduces him.)* A Maury from the Périgord. Come in, come in, my boy, these men are about to leave, you look frozen...

Simon nods. He rubs his hands and taps his feet.

POLICEMAN #1: *(buttoning up)* Winter's coming, no question.

MAURY: You can feel it in the air.

POLICEMAN #2: I like the cold.

MAURY: Really? That's unusual.

POLICEMAN #2: When there's a raw chill here and I'm freezing my butt off, I think of the Krauts who must be frozen stiff, over there, in Russia, and it warms my heart just thinking about it. *(He laughs.)* Ach, brr, brr!

Teeth chattering, knees shaking, he raises his arm, flashing the palm of his hand. Maury laughs.

POLICEMAN #1: *(to Maury, while readjusting his cap)* The day before yesterday we were in the area around Montillac, with the whole brigade, and some backup Militia and Mobile Reserve Units.

POLICEMAN #2: *(forging ahead)* Those guys, some kicks you

know where, is what they deserve...

POLICEMAN # 1: *(continuing)* We had a hell of a day... There was this guy yelling at us because he claimed we were rounding up other people's Jews but not his. The captain kept telling him there was nothing we could do since his Jews had their papers in perfect order, but he wouldn't back off. "It's always the big guys who win out in this country," he was yelling, "It's not fair, the Marshal should only know what goes on behind his back," and so on and so forth. In the end, just to shut him up, we rounded them up anyhow. I guess they handled it in Nexon. O.K., now, let's go.

MAURY: Well, then, have a good walk.

POLICEMAN #1: Thank you... Even the backroads around here are paved with rumors, so ...

MAURY: Well, try not to stumble over them.

POLICEMAN #1: *(agreeing gravely)* We'll try...

POLICEMAN #2: As long as there's no Militia or other phoney military people at our butt, we can still go our merry way, don't worry, we're fit as fiddles.

POLICEMAN #1: *(sententiously)* The overzealous incur God's wrath!

> *They all shake hands. The policemen exit. Simon is about to question Maury, but the latter immediately raises his index finger to his mouth, to silence him. The policemen can be heard walking away. After a brief silence, Maury rushes toward the door mumbling to Simon:*

MAURY: Terribly sorry, but I have to pee. *(He exits. Simon remains alone. He looks around and glances into the adjoining room. Maury can be heard yelling from the doorstep.)* Don't worry, Mr. Simon, don't worry...

> *Simon re-enters and exits to join Maury. The stage remains empty a moment, then blackout.*

SCENE 8

A winter night. The room is lit by a candle that sets the bottle and glass on the table aglow. Lea, barely visible, is huddled under a blanket on the otherwise bare bed. Simon, still wearing Maury's sheep-lined jacket, is seated at the table. Silence. After a moment, he serves himself and concentrates on his drink.

LEA: You coming to bed?

SIMON: No.

LEA: *(resuming)* It feels strange this way, with no one next door. *(Pause.)* But they'll be better off, won't they, with winter coming... And Maury's daughter-in-law said the people they're staying with are reliable. *(Silence.)* And us? *(Simon doesn't respond.)* Do you think we can stay here? *(Simon still doesn't respond, he pours himself another glassful and drinks.)* Why don't you say anything? Why are you drinking like that?

SIMON: Why, why... *(He slams the glass down on the table, and continues talking while striding up and down the room.)* Why'd you have to start selling your lousy shirts, eh? So that one of your "clients" could lose a button and inform on you for bad workmanship and illegal trade? Don't you understand that we have to lie low?

LEA: *(interrupting him)* Even if we lie low, we still have to eat, no?

SIMON: *(sitting down again)* True, we have to eat, I always forget that. Sorry. *(Silence again, then he resumes.)* Tell me— since you know everything—how can a blind man contribute to the great Reich's giant war effort?

LEA: Leave me alone, will you.

SIMON: Given his condition, I thought at least he'd still be there; and if Henri had stopped by... *(He stops.)*

LEA: *(more gently)* Simon, we've been through all this already...

SIMON: Right, I'm rambling, I can't get it out of my mind. *(Silence.)* What kind of country, State, or government, would charter special trains to import blind people who can't even restuff armchairs or tune their fabulous concert grands? What for, Lea, what for? His concierge told me that the cops had to carry him down the stairs. I can tell you when I had to take him to the eye clinic, or anywhere, I couldn't handle it, it made me sick at heart. And never in the world, Lea, would I have dreamt of taking a train trip with him. Though he's my favorite uncle... *(Silence.)* Apart from that, Lea, nothing has changed—Ramey, Labat and Simart streets, nothing. The oriental shop on Simart is still where it was. The name and the front haven't changed; they've just stuck a sign in the window, "Under French Management". *(He drinks again.)*

LEA: *(after a pause)* And what about our place? Did you go look?

SIMON: What for? To see the seals on the door, or the mugs of the new "French management"? *(Pause.)* Aunt Reizl is the only one who pulled a fast one on them. When they broke down her door, they found her laid out on the bed, her false teeth on the nighttable in a glass of water. *(He laughs.)* Imagine the expression on those officers' faces!...

She always had a knack for getting served before everyone! *(Pause.)* I don't know why, right before leaving I felt like going to Bagneux, to her grave, to meditate, as they say... But once I was there I didn't dare get near. I thought I'd no sooner set foot on our star-studded plot, than all the undertakers and keepers would surround me, ask me why I wasn't wearing a yellow star, pull my pants down and deliver me to the Gestapo. So I pretended I was interested in the countless deceased Duponts and Durands who are all over the place there, and I casually surveyed our two deserted gravesites out of the corner of my eye. Then suddenly I see this guy ambling over, a real caricature, Lea—an immediate incitement to a pogrom—beard, prayer shawl, black hat. On his threadbare coat, a gleaming yellow star, in full view, carefully sewn on. I hid behind the crosses and couldn't help staring at him... I was convinced he'd be caught any minute, that the whole German army and auxiliary forces—plus the Bagneux fire department—were hot on his trail, surrounding the cemetery, Montrouge, Paris and Ile-de-France and that I too was a dead duck, trapped at the center of the attack. All because of this wreck, this relic from the past, who didn't know how to dress or shave like everyone else. I started to run away, but ended up in an open pathway, halfway between the crosses and the stars. Thanks to his expert eye and ancestral flair, he had already grabbed me by the arm, called me his child and asked me in Yiddish if I wanted him to say a small prayer for me so my dear departed would rest in peace. He gripped my arm so tight, it felt like it was caught in a vise. It hurt, it hurt a lot. I couldn't breathe. I was suffocating. And then I recovered, and heard myself say, "Yes, I'd like that." A prayer, why not? It can't do any harm, but it can't do any good, or maybe it can. So I said: For my father... He asked me politely where my father's grave was and I said it was pretty far, over there, between Lemberg and Brody, in a little area whose name presently escaped me. He told me to go up to any grave and repeat after him. I repeated after him. He swayed back and forth and struck his breast. I swayed and struck myself. The grave belonged to a Mr. Elefant, whose passing would be forever mourned by his widow and children. Then I asked him, while he was at it, to say a small prayer on Mimé Reizl's grave, she who died in her bed, free, the night before a roundup. But I didn't know where her grave was, and I wasn't about to ask the keeper, which is what this lunatic was encouraging me to do in order to gain time. We went around in circles, both of us, looking and reading names. What magnificent names we have, Lea, endless like the sky, long, complicated, tortuous names, with difficult spellings for those who have to take a census and draw up lists before shipping us off. Finally I settled on the Future Brotherhood tomb—our tomb, Lea, our future, Lea. This is where he quickly mumbled a little prayer, though his heart wasn't in it anymore, he was already on the look-out, hoping to find another client. But the cemetery was deserted, it was the dead season. I gave him all my loose change and then, just to chat, I asked him if he came every day. No! Every other day he went to Pantin cemetery. Then he added, "We have to eat, no?" See, he too, he too. I felt like asking him what his rotten boss up there was up to, whether he'd gone bezerk or something, but I felt he was too bound by earthly matters, too worried about his meals, too starved for materiality to give me a serene answer, or even to serve as a disinterested intermediary. *(He stops for a second and then starts talking again.)* You know, if we make it...

LEA: We'll make it Simon, we'll make it...

SIMON: I won't go back to the treadmill. No. No more

packaging, delivering, invoicing, never. On Saturday night you won't catch me telling the usual old jokes at club dances, or hanging out and hailing a brighter tomorrow at those binges for Communist Party sympathizers. No...I'll learn a couple of prayers, really simple ones—like the ones for departed relatives—I'll let my beard grow, and every other day I'll traipse around Bagneux or Pantin, with a prayerbook under my arm, carefully wrapped in brown paper. And for a handful of change, I'll sway and beat my breast—assuming there are still some prayer buyers left—otherwise I'll do it for nothing, Lea, for nothing... *(Silence.)* Those who are gone won't return, Lea, and those who'll make it will have lost the zest for life. And if by some misfortune they have children, those children won't have a zest for life either, they'll be forever torn between Bagneux and Pantin; wherever they go they'll wear a big, cold, heavy tombstone around the neck engraved with the names of their relatives. I can already feel it, so cold and heavy. Right here! *(He touches his breast, like Apfelbaum, then continues.)* I heard from Maury that Apfelbaum and his family are in Nexon. *(After a pause.)* You mustn't stay here. You'll go join Mauricette or your mother. Maury and I discussed it this afternoon.

LEA: Me? You say me? What about you?

SIMON: I met a friend of Charles's in Paris, a former member of the Communist Youth movement. He helped me with food and so on, and he told me there's a Jewish resistance group in the country near Toulouse, veterans of the Immigrant Workers Movement.

LEA: You think Henri's there?

SIMON: *(surprised)* No... I don't think so Lea... Who can

think anything these days? *(He blows out the candle.)* I'm leaving tomorrow. *(He goes over to the bed in the dark and lies down. Lea starts sobbing. Simon gets up and walks over to the door, yelling.)* No, no, don't cry, goddamnit, don't cry!

> *He opens the door wide, and stands at the entrance, neither inside nor out, leaning against the doorpost, his back to the room and to Lea, and looks out into the night.*

LEA: *(from the bed)* There was no point in your coming back if you were going to leave again so soon! *(Simon doesn't react. Lea continues.)* You said yourself there are roadblocks everywhere and it's a miracle you made it!

SIMON: So what? So what? What am I supposed to do? What am I supposed to do?

LEA: Stay and wait! Wait with me until it's over! The Russians and Americans don't need your help. I do! I'm the only one who needs you!

SIMON: *(not letting her finish)* How long does a person live, Lea, how many years? How many days are there in a person's life...

> *He is interrupted by the rumbling of a plane above the house.*

LEA: *(yells, as the noise gets louder)* What is it?

SIMON: *(yells from outside)* Bombers, Lea, bombers!

LEA: *(yelling)* Simon, come inside right away! Come inside, do you hear?

Through the open door, Simon can be seen scaling up the embankment, waving his arms and yelling with joy. The sound of the planes reaches a peak, then fades away. Blackout.

SCENE 9

A spring afternoon. Sunshine streams in through the wide-open door and window. At center stage, the daughter-in-law, wearing a slip and high-heels obviously lent by Lea or Mauricette, is standing and waiting, arms crossed. Near her, Lea and Mauricette are almost finished basting the hem of a dress. Mrs. Schwartz can be seen outside through the open door, seated on her straw-bottomed armchair, facing the sun. She is wearing a strange hat. The daughter-in-law's child, barely older-looking than in scene two, is playing airplane, arms stretched out and humming noisily. He weaves back and forth, tirelessly, inside and outside. Occasionally he aims a burst of submachine gun fire or a bomb at one or another of the women present. However, his favorite target is his mother. She suddenly grabs him by the collar as he goes by, shakes him, and raises her other hand threateningly.

THE DAUGHTER-IN-LAW: That's enough! Or you'll get yours!

The child frees himself and resumes flying, firing a round of shots point blank at his mother. She tries to run after him, but the high heels make her unsteady. The child exits, forsaking aviation. Feigning fear, he takes refuge in Mrs. Schwartz's skirts. She willingly hides him and drives away the mother's threats with large gestures. Lea and Mauricette have finished basting the hem of the dress and both help the daughter-in-law slip it on. This is a solemn moment. The dress is made of shiny, satiny, ecru-colored fabric, with a full skirt. Once she is dressed, the daughter-

in-law dares not move. She looks questioningly at the two sisters, then mumbles:

THE DAUGHTER-IN-LAW: Do I look silly?

MAURICETTE: It's the fashion.

She walks around her, looking at her critically. Lea suddenly kneels down to correct the hemline.

LEA: It still hangs.

MAURICETTE: Because it gathers at the seams. Next time we'll tell the English to use real silk for their parachutes, it would fall better. *(All three laugh. To the daughter-in-law)* Walk a bit, Mrs. Maury, so we can see. *(The daughter-in-law takes one or two steps and imitating her son, even spreads out her arms and hums. Mauricette remains serious.)* Try and make the skirt fly instead.

THE DAUGHTER-IN-LAW: *(worried, stands still)* How? *(From where she is, Mauricette shows her by moving her hips slightly.)* Do I have to swing my hips?

MAURICETTE: *(demonstrating as she speaks)* No, take big steps as though you were very happy and in a hurry.

Mauricette demonstrates. The daughter-in-law tries, stops still and sits down in tears. After a brief moment, Lea kneels down beside her and awkwardly clasping her hands in hers, mumbles:

LEA: Come now, come now...

Mauricette walks away and goes to the door. She stays there, her back to the others. The child reappears and bumps into her; again he is playing airplane and enjoying shooting at his mother.

THE DAUGHTER-IN-LAW: *(to Lea, in a low voice, miserable)* Maybe it isn't very appropriate?

LEA: What isn't?

THE DAUGHTER-IN-LAW: Getting all dolled up. What will he think? That while he was eating grit in Silesia, my mind was on clothes!

LEA: *(whispering in her ear)* He won't think anything, he'll think you look beautiful.

The daughter-in-law hides her face in her hands and mumbles:

THE DAUGHTER-IN-LAW: I'm so afraid of seeing him again. *(At this point the kid knocks over a chair and drags it with him. Mauricette's baby can be heard waking up in the adjoining room. Mauricette rapidly crosses the room while the daughter-in-law runs after her son. She takes her shoes off, throws them at him and yells.)* Trouble-maker! Just you wait, I'll teach you, you little brat! *(The kid backs away toward the door, holding his elbows in. He is saved in the nick of time by the arrival of Maury and the two policemen, dressed partially in uniform, partially in civilian clothes. They are armed and look harassed. The three men are carrying pieces of a still. The daughter-in-law adjusts her posture and faces them, showing her dress with pride and confidence.)* So?

Policeman #1 puts the piece he is carrying on the table and gestures with his hand as a sign of complete exhaustion and disgust. Then he declares:

POLICEMAN #1: They say in Tulle they hanged all the men in the city.

THE DAUGHTER-IN-LAW: *(dumbfounded)* Who did?

MAURY: *(angry)* The Krauts of course! Who else?

Silence. The three men have put down the pieces of the still.

POLICEMAN #1: *(collapsing into a seat)* I can't take it anymore. My feet...

POLICEMAN #2: Plus everybody's on our backs! Unbelievable! The militia, the Gaullists, the commies, everyone! They all have it in for the police. Let's set up a roadblock, check I.D.s, look up your nose to see whose side you're on...

POLICEMAN #1: Civilian military are the worst! The worst!

Maury busies himself with his still. New silence. The daughter-in-law suddenly takes off her dress and hands it to Lea asking:

THE DAUGHTER-IN-LAW: Can it be dyed?

The policemen notice that she's in her slip and look away.

LEA: *(handing the dress to Mauricette)* Can it be dyed?

Mauricette fingers the dress, then takes it and brings it to her mother. She can be seen leaning towards her and talking. The mother fingers the dress. Mauricette comes back and says:

MAURICETTE: She says if you have dye it can be dyed.

THE DAUGHTER-IN-LAW: In black then, it'd be more suitable. *(Suddenly crackling is heard coming from the village below. The daughter-in-law looks worried.)* Now what?

POLICEMAN #2: *(at the doorstep)* Guingouin's men are returning to the village.

> *The sound of the* Marseillaise *can be heard indistinctly from far away.*

THE POLICEMEN: *(suddenly very moved)* Ladies, that's it, we're free!

> *The two policemen kiss the daughter-in-law while she struggles with her old blouse. They conscientiously kiss all the women present, with dignity, including Mrs. Schwartz. The sound of the* Internationale *is heard from a distance.*

MAURY: *(busying himself next to his still)* Time to stop dillydallying and get this thing working, seeing as when all our boys are back, people'll be real thirsty around here, right?

> *He turns to the ladies with a questioning look. Now Mauricette is crying in the daughter-in-law's arms. The latter pulls her into the adjoining room. The policemen, embarrassed, stretch out their arms, signifying that it isn't their fault. Maury shrugs his shoulders.*

POLICEMAN #1: *(whispering)* We'd better go.

POLICEMAN #2: Better show our faces, the reds are touchy!

MAURY: *(whispering as well)* Thanks for your help.

The two men protest, waving aside his thanks. They pick up their guns and leave on tiptoe. Maury busies himself with his still. The child is playing airplane again. In the adjoining room Mauricette is crying softly, while the baby is heard laughing, perhaps because the daughter-in-law is playing with her. The airplane-child disappears and joins his mother. Lea remains seated on the bed. Maury exits suddenly, very active. Lea drags an overnight bag across the floor, opens it and stands over it, arms hanging by her sides. Mrs. Schwartz is asleep in the setting sun.

SCENE 10

Early morning darkness broken by a flame burning under the still inside and a misty dawn outside. The place has changed, as though neglect had finally triumphed. Maury is spread out on the bare mattress, fully dressed. The remains of a meal are still on the table. Only the sewing machine, in its case, and the run-down baby carriage attest to the recent past. There is a knocking at the closed door. Maury turns over on the bed. More knocking, then the door is pushed open and Simon enters. He is still wearing Maury's sheep-lined jacket, but with an undershirt underneath. His trousers, shoes and bundle make him look like a vagabond. He has a rifle on his shoulder and is holding an American army flashlight. He bumps into the still.

SIMON: *(complaining)* What the hell is this mess?

MAURY: *(sitting up in bed and brandishing a stick)* Who goes there?

SIMON: *(aiming his flashlight at Maury)* What are you doing here?

MAURY: Well, well! This is my place, isn't it? *(He covers his eyes.)* Turn that off!

SIMON: Where are they?

MAURY: In Limoges.

SIMON: In Limoges?

MAURY: Your mother-in-law couldn't stand the country

anymore. *(He raises his arms then lets them fall.)* So...

Simon nods and in the same breath says:

SIMON: And Henri?

> *Maury lowers his head. Simon nods again then sits down at the table and takes a piece of bread that is lying around.*

MAURY: I have some salami. *(He gets up and takes a salami, wrapped in a checkered handkerchief, out of his pocket. He carefully unfolds the cloth. Then, taking out his pocket knife, he ceremoniously cuts a few slices. Simon eats, with quasi-religious concentration. Maury sits down opposite him.)* So you're a hero now? You liberated Toulouse?

SIMON: *(while eating)* Didn't liberate anything, they thought I was too old to see gunfire. In all my life I've never sewed so many buttons and peeled so many potatoes. War's for the young.

MAURY: Not just war, from what they say...

SIMON: *(nodding and repeating)* Not just war... *(Pause.)* Why're we speaking in a low voice?

MAURY: Yes? Why? Well, I guess 'cause there's nothing to shout about.

SIMON: *(putting down his piece of bread, gets up, listens a moment, then mumbles)* You're pulling my leg, right? You're pulling my leg. They're here. Lea? *(He walks over to the adjoining room, but Maury hurriedly blocks the way. Simon stops in front of him, surprised and worried.)* What's going on?

MAURY: I'll tell you...

SIMON: What are you going to tell me?

MAURY: Nothing. I'll explain, that's all. When your ladies left, you see, it created something of a void. And then, seeing as the son's missis and me don't really get along anymore, because of her husband, my son, you see, who's on his way back, she was climbing the walls, it was driving her nuts. So I decided to head back to my dug-out. There. If you have a porcupine on your butt it's best not to sit, right?

SIMON: *(listening and pointing to the adjoining room)* Someone's sleeping there!

MAURY: I'm coming to that, I tell you... Just listen. O.K. Once I was here alone—I mean all alone—I couldn't stand it. And since the Resistance, mind you, had prisoners who had to be put up with reliable people, I went to the town hall and took one. That's all.

SIMON: *(after a pause)* I don't understand.

MAURY: There's nothing to understand.

SIMON: There's a German here?

MAURY: *(as though he were holding back laughter)* Right. *(Silence. Still as though he were holding back laughter.)* Only I wasn't lucky, ever since he's been here he's been crying all the time, except when he's sleeping of course.

SIMON: He cries?

MAURY: Right. From what I understand, he hasn't heard from his parents for a while.

SIMON: No kidding...

MAURY: He thinks they were blown up during the bombings.

SIMON: And that's a reason to cry?

Silence.

MAURY: So last night, see, I used emergency measures, I gave him a huge dose, until he was rolling under the table. Me too, I must say, I... *(He holds his head. Simon cocks his rifle, heads straight for the door, and runs straight into Maury. The latter blocks the doorway, clutching the frame, unwilling to yield his ground.)* What exactly do you think you're doing?

SIMON: Relieving him of the urge to cry.

MAURY: *(standing up straight)* Be careful, huh, he's my prisoner, my prisoner! The underground put him in my care!

SIMON: I have a cure-all that's a heck of a lot more powerful than yours. Come on, be nice Maury, get out of my way.

MAURY: Not a chance, you'd have to knock me off first!

SIMON: So what? I've got several cartridges. And I've finally learned how to use this thing. I even know how to recharge it.

MAURY: You've really lost your marbles!

SIMON: Wrong, I've gone completely normal, you're the one who's old-hat, dated, one war behind the times. What's one more life for us humans? Prisoners, honor, hospitality—that's all over! First in line to be killed are women and children, the elderly and the disabled!

MAURY: *(interrupting him forcefully)* No, sir, no, not in my house!

SIMON: Even in your lousy house, what do you think? God in his infinite kindness wanted to round things off by giving me this little opportunity—a discreet, domestic opportunity—of becoming a full-fledged human being like everyone else. Come on, move out of the way, hero of the great war, this war's for civilians, not soldiers. *(He places the barrel of the rifle on Maury's chest.)*

MAURY: Son of bitch! I'll show you! *(He grabs the barrel and yells as he presses it against his chest.)* Well, go on! Shoot! Shoot!

SIMON: *(trying to free the rifle)* Let go, let go, I tell you! *(They fight for possession of the rifle and suddenly it goes off. They are startled, exhausted and panicked, and they both step back. The rifle lies at their feet between them. Maury collapses in the doorway, Simon is next to the table. At this point a very youthful-looking young man appears at Maury's back, in combat fatigues, disheveled and stunned. He looks at the two men in surprise. Simon raises his eyes and looks at him, then looks away mumbling.)* A child, goddamnit...

> *Maury stands up and places his hand on the prisoner's shoulder.*

MAURY: He'll help me in the fields.

SIMON: *(still looking away)* You work in the fields these days?

MAURY: He'll play dominoes with me, drink the potion, pick the different herbs, inherit the secret of...of Vercingetorix. And after a year or two, he'll go back to his native Krautland, right numbskull? Good schlafen sie?

The German nods. He is sad.

SIMON: This is hard to believe. We no sooner turn our backs and there's a Kraut in our place...

MAURY: Hey, hey! This here is my place! Got it? And families of penniless Kikes don't turn up every day of the week. No such luck. You have to take what comes, the hoi-polloi, and make do... And besides what do you expect? Everyone's leaving, they're not even waiting for Paris to surrender, they're off, so long, bye bye, everyone's gone. So I should just stay all by myself? Well, no, that's over, I won't stay alone again, no sir, never again. *(The young German asks Maury in German if Simon is his son. Worried, Maury quizzes Simon.)* What's he saying?

SIMON: Go to hell.

MAURY: Thank you, thank you very much.

SIMON: *(reluctantly)* He wants to know if we're father and son.

MAURY: Not on your life! An ass like you! *(The young German exits and returns with a camera. He asks in German if he can take a souvenir picture of father and son.)* What's he saying now?

SIMON: *(still without looking at them)* He wants a souvenir picture of father and son.

Outside day has dawned.

MAURY: Please tell him I'm not your father and you're not my son. Tell him.

Roosters are heard.

SIMON: Relay your own messages. *(He stands up.)*

MAURY: *(to Simon, after staring at the German)* This morning, he looks better, doesn't he? The potion seems to work.

SIMON: What did she say?

MAURY: Who?

SIMON: Lea, my wife, did she say anything concerning me?

MAURY: Yes, yes...

SIMON: So why didn't you tell me! Why are you breaking my balls with your stories?

MAURY: She said that... that... she'd stop by the Limoges station every day between five and six and if you missed each other in Limoges, she'd be in Paris, either at Charles', or at Leon's, or...

SIMON: Or?

MAURY: Damn it, damn it, I'm fed up being an inter-mediary. I forgot.

SIMON: I agree, intermediaries should be eliminated.

MAURY: I approve, a hundred percent, eliminate inter-mediaries.

SIMON: Between five and six, at the Limoges station... *(He has difficulty breathing.)*

MAURY: She also said you should take the sewing machine.

SIMON: What?

MAURY: She took all your belongings. The sewing machine was too heavy. She's counting on you.

SIMON: She's out of her mind! That old contraption isn't even ours.

MAURY: Compliments of the house!

SIMON: If you think I'm going to drag that relic around.

MAURY: Leave it, I don't care... I'm only relaying what she told me to tell you.

SIMON: *(lifting the machine in its case)* Oh, damn it, hell...

> He sits down, exhausted, and hides his face momentarily, turning his back to Maury. The German asks what's going on in German.

MAURY: What's he saying?

SIMON: Hell! It's going to be great when you two are all alone!

MAURY: Oh, we understand each other, we understand each other... but right now, we don't have time. *(Simon walks back to the sewing machine and hesitates.)* Wouldn't you like to take a little rest? The Kraut and I are going out to pick herbs, right numbskull? Ya, ya, nature gutt... When we get back I'll make us a little omelette with chives. *(Simon suddenly hugs Maury and lingers in his arms a moment. Maury waits for him to recover; the German takes the opportunity to photograph them. Simon lifts the sewing machine and Maury says, very straightforwardly:)* I'd be much obliged to you if you could return my jacket. I could still get some wear out of it around here. *(Simon puts down the sewing machine, takes off the jacket, and throws it on the table. Maury takes out Simon's carefully folded coat from under the bed.)* Here it is.

SIMON: Keep it.

MAURY: No, no.

SIMON: It's too hot, it's either the coat or the sewing machine! Not both, not both!

MAURY: *(hugging the coat)* O.K., I'll put it away for you, you'll be back?

SIMON: Never.

MAURY: Aren't you going to say goodbye to the son's missis?

SIMON: *(yelling)* No!

He walks up the embankment lugging the sewing machine, his bundle hanging from his other shoulder.

MAURY: *(notices the rifle on the ground, picks it up and exits, yelling)* Hey, your gun! *(No response. Simon has vanished. Maury re-enters, throws the rifle into the baby carriage, then says:)* That's it!

Black out.

"Today I am giving myself to France to alleviate her misfortune"
—Marshal Pétain, June 17, 1940

J'AI ÉTÉ
AVEC VOUS
DANS LES JOURS
GLORIEUX

JE RESTE
AVEC VOUS
DANS LES JOURS
SOMBRES...

SERVIR

1918

1940

I was with you in
the days of glory

I remain with you
in the dark days

"They built your country". Top left: Richelieu; top right: Saint-Louis; bottom left: Sully; bottom right: Colbert.

"The Little Yid. When he comes of age, he will use his money and connections to be classified unfit instead of doing his military service. Because he is a Jew!

But! One day, the people—fed up, perspicacious and furious—will throw this parasite out of our country. And that day everyone will celebrate....because there will be no more Jews".

*A Vichy government postcard promoting the values of its "National Revolution".
On the left: Laziness, Demagogy, Internationalism; on the right: Work, Family,
Country.*

"Jewish business". Sign posted on the door of a store in Paris.

Map showing the demarcation line and the principal internment camps for Jews in the occupied and unoccupied zones, 1941.

Roundup of Jews in Paris, August, 1941.

Jewish men at the Gare d'Austerlitz in Paris preparing to board trains for the camps at Pithiviers and Beaune-la-Rolande, August, 1941.

Newly arriving Jews being registered at the Pithiviers camp.

First day at the Pithiviers camp.

116

The Drancy camp.

Work duty at Drancy.

On May 29, 1942, it became mandatory for Jews to wear a yellow star in the occupied zone.

118

"Against Communism: The French Militia"

"To live free or die." The cross of Lorraine, symbol of the Resistance.

119

A toute heure du jour, les chasseurs britanniques effectuent des balayages au-dessus de la France occupée, acclamés par les paysans français

British poster, 1942.
"British fighter planes conduct hourly
raids over occupied France, to the acclaim
of the French peasants."

The city of Castres, in Southern France, liberated by a detachment of Jewish
Resistance fighters.

COMMEMORATIVE PLAQUE ON THE FACADE OF THE HOTEL LUTETIA:
"Between April and August 1945, many of the survivors of Nazi
concentration camps were received in this hotel which had been
transformed into a welcoming center. They were very happy to find
freedom again, and the loved ones from whom they had been torn away.
Their joy failed to erase the anguish and sorrow of the families of the
thousands of dead who awaited in vain for their relatives here at this site.
40th anniversary of the liberation of the camps. May 21, 1985".

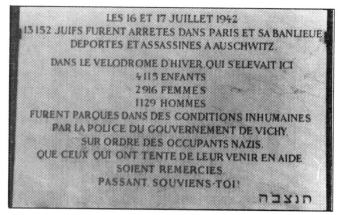

COMMEMORATIVE PLAQUE ON THE SITE OF THE VÉLODROME D'HIVER:
"On July 16th and 17th, 1942, 13,152 Jews were arrested in Paris and
suburbs, then deported and murdered in Auschwitz. In the Vélodrome
d'hiver that stood here, 4,115 children, 2,916 women and 1,129 men
were kept in inhuman conditions by Vichy government police under
orders from the Nazi occupants. May those who tried to help them be
thanked. In passing by, remember!"

Jean-Claude Grumberg

THE
WORKROOM

Translated from the French
by **Catherine Temerson**

Ubu Repertory Theater Publications
NEW YORK

INTRODUCTION

The first workroom of my life was the unused area in the three-room apartment of my childhood where my father used to work before the war. In the 1950's my mother finally decided to turn it into a room for my brother and me. Waiting for my father to return, she worked as a finisher in a workroom for ready-made men's wear. Later – we were no longer waiting, having gradually learned the meaning of the word "deported"– I myself became a tailor's apprentice and came to know other workrooms...

This play is written for my mother, and for all the women and men whom I saw laugh and cry in the many workrooms I have known.

JEAN-CLAUDE GRUMBERG
1979

CHARACTERS

Hélène

Simone

Gisèle

Marie

Madame Laurence

Mimi

Léon

First Presser

Jean, Second Presser

Sewing Machine Operator #1

Sewing Machine Operator #2

The Child

SCENE 1

THE TRYOUT

1945. Very early morning. Simone is sitting at the table working, her back to the audience. Standing by another table, Hélène , the owner's wife, is also working. From time to time she glances at Simone.

HELENE: My sister, too, they took her in '43...

SIMONE: She came back?

HELENE: No... She was twenty-two. *(Silence.)* Did you run your own business?

SIMONE: Yes, just me and my husband. We used to hire a girl for the busy season... last month I had to sell the machine. He won't be able to start working again... I shouldn't have, but...

HELENE: Sewing machines aren't that hard to come by...

SIMONE: *(nodding in approval)* I shouldn't have sold it but I was offered coal and...

 Silence.

HELENE: You have children?

SIMONE: Yes, two boys...

HELENE: How old?

SIMONE: Ten and six.

HELENE: That's a good age difference... Or so they say... I don't have children...

SIMONE: They make out all right. The older boy takes care of his little brother. They were in the country, in the free zone. When they returned, he had to explain to him who I was. He hid behind his big brother and didn't want to look at me. He called me "Madame"...

She laughs. Gisèle has just entered. She stops briefly at the clothesrack which the presser uses to hang up the pieces he's just ironed and which the women workers use as a coatrack. She removes her jacket, hangs it, puts on her smock and goes to her seat. She greets Simone and Madame Hélène with a nod. Hélène introduces the women to each other.

HELENE: Madame Gisèle... Madame Simone, for the finishing work.

Gisèle nods in approval. She and Simone nod at each other again and smile. Gisèle is already at work. Enter Madame Laurence, immediately followed by Marie. They both greet Madame Hélène, in ringing voices.

MADAME LAURENCE AND MARIE: Good morning, Madame Hélène.

They change into their smocks. Marie is still buttoning her smock as she starts work on her first piece; Madame Laurence takes her time, removing her shoes and slipping into felt slippers. She shuffles slowly to her place at the end of the table, facing Simone, her back to the window on a tall stool. There she can dominate. Hélène continues to work as she introduces the women. Simone smiles at each of the newcomers. Now all four are working silently, each at her own pace. Standing in front of her table, Hélène is basting the cloth on the fronts of jackets; she works at great speed, glancing occasionally at the workers. Enter Mimi, breathless. She is immediately greeted by Gisèle's remark.

GISELE: You fall out of bed again this morning?

While slipping on her smock, Mimi gestures with her hand as though to say, "don't ask." Hélène then introduces her.

HELENE: Miss Mimi... Madame Simone.

Simone smiles at Mimi. As she sits down, Mimi extends her hand ceremoniously to Simone. The latter sticks her needle into her piece and shakes hands with her, thereby hindering Marie who grumbles. Mimi glances at Marie contemptuously but says nothing. As soon as Mimi starts working Madame Laurence moves her stool back a bit and addresses her.

MADAME LAURENCE: One day you'll poke out my eye...

Mimi doesn't respond; she's at work. Silence. Gisèle starts humming without thinking.

HELENE: Feeling good today, Madame Gisèle!

GISELE: *(surprised)* Me? No. Why?

HELENE: I hear you humming, so...

GISELE: Humming? Me? I'm not humming, Madame Hélène . My heart isn't in it, not these days.

Tears well up in her eyes. Mimi and Marie look at her and break out laughing.

MADAME LAURENCE: *(looking over at Simone's work and addressing her)* You used to do quality work? *(Simone nods.)* I can tell. Those nice little stitches...

> *The boss, Monsieur Léon, suddenly sticks his head through the door that leads to the other workrooms. He appears for an instant and calls out very loudly twice.*

LEON: Hélène ! Hélène !

> *All the women start, let out a cry of fear, then break out laughing. Hélène sighs. Léon can be heard losing his temper in the adjoining room—possibly on the phone. The sound of the machines is distinctly heard. Madame Laurence shakes her head, holding her bosom. Simone, who was as startled as the others, laughs heartily. Mimi imitates the bark and growl of a dog as Madame Hélène exits, shutting the door behind her. They can be heard talking and then walking away.*

GISELE: Well, the day's off to a good start... Yelling first thing in the morning, I... *(She doesn't finish her sentence.)*

MADAME LAURENCE: I smell trouble...

SIMONE: Is he always like that?

MADAME LAURENCE: Monsieur Léon? You haven't met him yet? We'll let you find out for yourself...

MIMI: *(hoarse, almost voiceless)* It will be repeated.

MADAME LAURENCE: What will?

MIMI: *(still hoarse and remaining so until the end of the scene)*

I'll repeat to Monsieur Léon what you said about him.

MADAME LAURENCE: *(turning to the others for support)* You out of your head? The girl has lost her marbles. What did I say? What did I say? *(Mimi clears her throat without answering. Marie is trying hard not to laugh. Madame Laurence glares at her.)* What's so funny?

MARIE: It's her voice... *(She bursts out laughing. To Mimi)* It's your voice.

MIMI: *(after clearing her throat)* So you think it's funny, wiseguy? *(Marie nods. Meanwhile Gisèle has advised Simone to take a place closer to the window, between her and Madame Laurence, so she can have more light. Simone has thanked Gisèle and changed places, with Gisèle's help. Simone now faces Mimi. Noticing her, Mimi continues talking.)* Fools always laugh at other people's misfortunes...

Marie thanks her while laughing.

GISELE: Might as well laugh it makes up for the meat shortage...

Mimi coughs; Simone rummages through her handbag and takes out a box of throat lozenges which she hands to her.

SIMONE: It's good for the throat...

MIMI: *(helping herself)* Thank you..

Simone offers them to the others who help themselves.

MARIE: *(reading)* "Cachou medicated lozenges ease

coughing and sweeten the breath."

GISELE: You can tell who has children... *(Simone nods.)* How many?

SIMONE: Two.

GISELE: An armful, huh?

MIMI: *(interrupting her)* Why don't you ever give out candy? You're a mom, too, aren't you?

GISELE: I don't even give any to my own kids. You can't exactly expect me to buy some specially for you?

MIMI: Yes I can, it would make me happy... You never give us anything...

> *Gisèle remains speechless.*

MADAME LAURENCE: *(to Mimi)* You'd better abstain today, let your organ rest for once... *(Mimi snickers and quavers. Madame Laurence continues.)* It's for your own sake. Of course if you think what you have to say is so important... *(Brief silence. She resumes.)* One day of quiet wouldn't exactly... *(Nimbly and unobtrusively, Mimi had brought her stool closer to Madame Laurence's. The latter finds herself once again bothered by Mimi's arm and threatened by her needle. Madame Laurence cuts herself off, moves back slightly, then resumes with a dignified air.)* Would you mind leaving me a bit of breathing space?

GISELE AND MARIE: *(together)* My dear...

MIMI: What's she saying? *(Madame Laurence sets the piece she has finished down next to her, rises and exits. Mimi struggles to speak to all present.)* She's taking a leak earlier than usual, a plumber should plug it up...

> *But her voice falters. She clears her throat and coughs. Simone takes out her box again. Mimi turns her down with a gesture.*

GISELE: *(dryly, to Simone)* You'd be wiser to keep them for your kids.

MARIE: *(after thumping Mimi's back)* How'd you come down with this?

MIMI: *(shrugging her shoulders)* I don't know... I went dancing last night and afterwards I got soaked...

GISELE: Did it rain last night?

MIMI: *(shaking her head)* I fell into the gutter. *(Marie bursts out laughing.)* Go on, have your kicks... I was with Huguette, my friend Huguette...

GISELE: The fat one.

MIMI: She isn't that fat...

GISELE: Isn't Huguette the one you call "the fat cow"?

MIMI: *(nodding)* That's right, but that doesn't mean she's fat. She just looks fat... Yesterday we went to the dance hall together. I took off my shoes to dance and when it was over I couldn't find them...

> *Marie is in stitches. Simone starts chuckling as well.*

GISELE: You lost your shoes?

MIMI: Someone swiped them, that 's what...

GISELE: People now take off their shoes to dance?

MIMI: The swing... to dance the swing... So two Yankees kindly offered to walk us home; one of them carried me so I wouldn't dirty my little footsies and then I don't know what they jabbered about but at one point one of them asked me something—I couldn't understand what—but I nodded and so did my friend, and without warning the guy dumped me into the gutter. I was drenched and then Huguette and the two Yanks start cracking up so we got into an argument. *(She clears her throat, struggling more and more.)* This morning I woke up like this; I couldn't talk at all...

> *Gisèle, Marie and Simone are in stitches.*

MADAME LAURENCE: *(re-enters and returns to her seat, then talks)* Am I the butt of the joke? *(Gisèle, Marie and Simone shake their heads and laugh even harder. Madame Laurence addresses Simone who tries to stop laughing out of politeness to her.)* You've caught on real fast; it doesn't matter, I'm used to it; she sets everyone up against me.

> *Simone is unable to quiet down. Her increasingly nervous laugh is punctuated with apologies.*

GISELE: *(to Madame Laurence)* We didn't say anything about you, not a thing...

MIMI: *(to Gisèle)* Come on... It's not nice to tell a lie, since we said, especially her... *(She points to Gisèle. Simone now has*

136

a handkerchief in her hand. She has stopped working and is dabbing her eyes as she continues to excuse herself with each outburst of laughter. Mimi continues.) That's what happens when you don't understand Yankee talk. Huguette said I shouldn't have nodded. *(She pronounces a sentence in "American".)*

MARIE: Were they drunk or what?

GISELE: So you came home drenched and barefoot?

MIMI: *(now laughing herself)* My skirt was sticking to me on all sides... It shrank. Real junk that crappy bonded fiber...

> *They all laugh again except Madame Laurence who is sulking conspicuously. Little by little, calm returns.*

GISELE: How can you go out dancing like that every night?

MIMI: I don't go every night. I went last night...

MARIE: *(to Simone)* You go dancing too?

> *Simone shakes her head, laughing.*

GISELE: She said she had children.

MARIE: So? Women with children aren't allowed? *(Gisèle shakes her head in annoyance.)* Some women even go dancing with their husband, don't they?

SIMONE: *(merely to cut the conversation short)* These days, I don't go dancing.

GISELE: See!

MARIE: Is it because your husband doesn't like to?

SIMONE: *(after a slight pause)* He's not here. He's been deported.

> *Brief silence.*

MIMI: *(still in a hoarse voice)* When I think about it, what a bastard that Yankee was... Maybe he's the one who swiped my shoes...

GISELE: Serves you right, you shouldn't take them off... Really, I've never...

MIMI: *(cutting her off)* Did you use to dance?

GISELE: Of course.

MIMI: No kidding!

GISELE: When I was a young...

MIMI: You were once young? No kidding?

GISELE: Anyway, I can tell you I never danced with servicemen.

MARIE: Why not, if they're not Krauts?

GISELE: Say what you will, there are certain things Krauts wouldn't do... *(She turns toward Simone.)* I'm sorry, I mean sometimes Americans can be... *(She stops.)*

MIMI: *(after a pause)* Go on, spill it out, tell all...

MADAME LAURENCE: What exactly were you driving at Madame Gisèle?

GISELE: Nothing, nothing...

MADAME LAURENCE: *(conciliatory)* You preferred having the Germans to the Americans?

GISELE: That's not what I said. Don't put words into my mouth...

MADAME LAURENCE: *(increasingly conciliatory)* as far as manners are concerned of course.

GISELE: For proper behavior, maybe, though it's like with everything, huh...

MIMI: You want us to invite them back? You miss the Krauts, do you?

> *She whistles to all present. Gisèle shrugs her shoulders. Silence.*

MADAME LAURENCE: The fact is, when the Americans weren't here we were praying for them to come. Now they're here, and we're practically praying for them to leave.

MIMI: Speak for yourself. They don't bother me. Except when they swipe my shoes and dump me in the water.

MADAME LAURENCE: I think they're a bit lacking in...

MARIE: Was one of them lacking in respect towards you, Madame Laurence?

Mimi shrieks with laughter. Madame Laurence shrugs her shoulders. The door opens. Madame Hélène calls out.

HELENE: Madame Simone, please. *(Simone rises and puts down her piece. Hélène continues from the door.)* No, no, bring it along...

Hélène disappears. Simone seems nervous.

GISELE: Did you discuss money yet? *(Simone shakes her head.)* Don't let yourself be cowed...

MARIE: *(whispering to Simone as she passes by)* Watch out. He's grasping, like a crab...

Simone exits.

MADAME LAURENCE: *(to Marie)* What did you say?

MARIE: When?

MADAME LAURENCE: You mentioned crab?

MARIE: I said he's grasping, like a crab.

MADAME LAURENCE: *(after a small pause)* I don't get it.

Marie shrugs her shoulders.

GISELE: Still, he's nice.

MARIE: *(annoyed)* All the same...

Silence.

MIMI: *(to Marie)* Her too.

MARIE: What?

MIMI: *(pointing to Simone's stool)* Her too...

MARIE: Her too what?

Mimi traces the outline of a big nose.

MARIE: You're crazy.

MIMI: Right!

MARIE: I don't think...

MIMI: I can tell. Right off the bat. I can tell.

Marie shrugs her shoulders.

GISELE: Anyway, she's nice!

MIMI: Oh boy, I don't believe it. Everyone sure is nice to her this morning...

GISELE: I like her, that's all.

MIMI: Well so do I like her. But the fact is, she too, she's...

MADAME LAURENCE: She has a funny laugh!

Silence.

GISELE: The poor thing probably hasn't had the opportunity to laugh too often recently, given all her misfortunes.

MIMI: So? We all have our misfortunes. I lost my shoes. I

don't go around making...

GISELE: *(to Marie, reproachfully)* And you went and asked her if her husband likes to dance.

MARIE: How was I supposed to know?

MADAME LAURENCE: There are some things you can sense...

> *Marie has finished her piece. She cuts off her ticket, puts it away in her box and looks around. She is angry.*

MARIE: I've no more work!

GISELE: Go and get some.

MARIE: *(remaining seated)* I'm not required...

GISELE: You prefer to lose a piece rather than move your ass?

MARIE: If I do it once I'll have to do it all the time... But how come I have no more work?

> *Simone has returned and is back at her seat.*

GISELE: *(to Simone)* So?

SIMONE: O.K. I think it'll be O.K.

MADAME LAURENCE: Did you hit it off with him? *(Simone looks at her without understanding.)* Did you get what you wanted?

142

SIMONE: Yes, well, nothing special. What you'd expect...

GISELE: You'll see, everything will be fine. Here there's work all year around.

MARIE: *(increasingly annoyed)* There's work everywhere these days.

GISELE: Exactly, all the more reason. Here too!

MARIE: So, what did you think of our monkey?

SIMONE: O.K. Well, nothing special...

MIMI: *(to Simone)* You'd better make bigger stitches or you'll never make it. Stretch them out a bit. Otherwise...

HELENE: *(who just entered, to Mimi)* Count on you for useful advice, Miss Mimi.

MIMI: *(bursting out laughing)* I didn't hear you come in, Madame Hélène. You'd better keep your wooden shoes for work and your rubber ones for Sundays.

MARIE: Madame Hélène , I've finished my piece and...

Enter Léon. He is very nervous.

LEON: *(to Hélène)* So, did you tell them?

HELENE: No, I just walked in...

LEON: So what are you waiting for?

HELENE: *(sighing)* I was about to tell them. I just walked in...

GISELE: What's going on Monsieur Léon?

LEON: She'll tell you, she'll tell you... *(He exits.)*

HELENE: *(calling him back)* Since you're here now you tell them yourself.

LEON: *(from the adjoining room)* I told you to tell them. So don't tell me to tell them...

HELENE: *(addressing the women workers as she bustles about the workroom and tidies it up)* We didn't get the fabric they were supposed to deliver, so Monsieur Léon couldn't cut... The guys are going home... Anyway, finish what you're working on and go home.

MARIE: What? *(Hélène has already exited.)* What did she say?

GISELE: Boy, that's something... What am I going to do all afternoon?

MIMI: You'll go home, to your dearly beloved...

GISELE: If you think it's funny...

MARIE: Get a load of that: he didn't get the fabric and we're left high and dry. He doesn't give a hoot that we've come here for nothing. I come from the other end of Paris to get here. "Go home!" They're really well organized, it's scary.

MADAME LAURENCE: Well, ladies, I'm calling it a day.

> She rises, puts her scissors away in her box and slips the box into the drawer.

Marie and Mimi exit arm in arm. Marie is still grumbling. Mimi imitates her and laughs. Gisèle and Simone remain seated, side by side. They complete their work in silence.

SCENE 2

SONGS

1946. Shortly before noon. All the women workers are present. The presser is at his pressing table. Gisèle has a headache. She takes a pill.

MIMI: What's wrong?

GISELE: I've a headache.

SIMONE: You'll survive.

Gisèle tries to swallow the pill. She makes several attempts.

MIMI: It won't go down? *(Gisèle shakes her head and takes another sip of water.)* Uptight airhole!

Marie laughs.

GISELE: *(to Marie)* Oh, please...

MARIE: What? We have no right to laugh?

GISELE: Not incessantly.

MARIE: With you it averages out.

GISELE: I'd like to see what you'd do in my shoes... *(She starts working again.)*

MIMI: Come on, stop thinking about it...

GISELE: Stop thinking about... I've a headache, I tell you...

146

MIMI: Sing us a song. That'll get your mind off it. *(They all urge her. Gisèle shakes her head without answering.)* Don't be mean, damn it...

GISELE: I don't feel like singing.

MIMI: For me, my pet...

MADAME LAURENCE: She likes to be begged...

GISELE: Well, why don't you sing yourself...

MADAME LAURENCE: If I were gifted, like you, I'd be happy to...

GISELE: Right... Don't butter me up...

MIMI: *(humming)* "I have two big oxen in my shed"... Go on, sing... *(She starts humming again.)* "Two big white oxen..."

GISELE: If I owned two oxen I wouldn't be here... *(After a pause.)* The butcher shops will be closing three days a week...

MADAME LAURENCE: Not for everyone. The front door, but not the back door...

MIMI: *(singing)* "Back to front, front to back/sadly, without fuss or airs/She knew love".

While Mimi sings, Gisèle pursues her thoughts.

GISELE: True, some people are never deprived of anything.

MADAME LAURENCE: *(carefully enunciating her words)*

There's plenty around, but not for everybody!

GISELE: I wonder what it takes...

MARIE: Hey ho, can't we change the subject?

GISELE: I'd like to see you what you'd do in my shoes...

MARIE: I'm not in the same boat?

GISELE: You don't have children!

MARIE: So? Neither does Madame Laurence... Or Mimi...

GISELE: It's easier if you're young, you know... *(Brief pause.)* Less bread than in '43!

SIMONE: Their bread is lousy...

GISELE: No question. They're terrific at food distribution..

SIMONE: It was lousy during the war too.

GISELE: Yes, but then there was the war...

Silence.

MADAME LAURENCE: What could I make Saturday that's both good and filling?

MIMI: Horse balls...

MADAME LAURENCE: Come on...

MIMI: Well? They're good and they're filling...

MADAME LAURENCE: There'll be eight of us. My husband's invited...

MIMI: *(interrupting her)* Buy two pairs...

> *Silence.*

GISELE: True, you and your husband...

MADAME LAURENCE: What about my husband?

MIMI: He gets laborer's rations, doesn't he?

MADAME LAURENCE: He has the same rights as everyone else... the same rights...

> *Gisèle is on the verge of saying something, but checks herself. She sighs, looks down, concentrating on her work. Silence. Still working, head bowed, Gisèle starts singing to herself, without thinking, in a low voice. Mimi signals to the others and starts accompanying her softly in a grotesque manner. Gisèle immediately stops singing and silence reigns again.*

MIMI: So, Gis old kid? Come on?

GISELE: Think I don't know when I'm being made fun of?

MIMI: I'm singing the second voice so it'll sound prettier.

GISELE: Thanks.

> *They all urge her again. Gisèle refuses, silently and obstinately.*

MIMI: *(suggesting)* Gis, we'll all turn away so you won't be embarrassed. Even the presser. O.K., presser sweetheart. Turn away, will you? Don't look at the performer. Come on, girls, turn away. Good... *(They all turn away. Mimi continues, looking at the presser.)* See, this way we're not even looking at you and I won't do the second voice since you don't like it.

> *Silence. Everything is still. They are all turning away. Only Gisèle is in her usual position. She seems determined not to sing. The women continue working. They reach gropingly for the scissors or spools on the table without turning toward Gisèle. The presser continues ironing, his head barely turned away. Suddenly Gisèle starts up. She sings a very sentimental song in a strong, resonant voice. Marie and Mimi refrain from laughing for as long as they can. Finally they succumb, causing Madame Laurence to laugh as well, and then Simone. But Gisèle has already stopped in the middle of a note. She is now working silently, with irrepressible energy.*

MIMI: Well, why'd you stop? *(Gisèle doesn't reply.)* What's wrong now?

GISELE: I'm being laughed at...

MIMI: Not at all, in fact we were deeply moved...

GISELE: *(pointing at Marie with her scissors)* Her, her... She's laughing at me... *(Marie bursts out laughing.)* Oh, sure, it isn't swing, it isn't hip... *(She hums menacingly.)* "There are hipsters in my neighborhood, bang, bang, tra la la, boom, boom." That's nice, real fine.

MARIE: Did I say anything?

GISELE: As soon as I start singing, she laughs at me, so...
Sing that jitterbug crap yourself instead of making others
sing. Poking fun is easy...

She imitates another hip song in a nasal voice.

MARIE: What's with her?

MIMI: Yeah, what's with you, Gis? Why are you so touchy?
Did you eat tigermeat?

GISELE: This is why everything's a mess right now.
Anything's good for a laugh. You go around yelping and
wiggling like animals who've escaped from the zoo. No
respect for anything. Even the quality of the work's gone
downhill...

Mimi whistles the tune that Gisèle gave up singing.

MARIE: *(to Gisèle)* Mind repeating what you said?

GISELE: Young people don't even know how to sew
anymore. That's what I was saying. And, believe me, I'm
not the only one to say so...

MARIE: *(half standing)* Cut it out, will you, cut it out...

GISELE: Listen, you little twerp... It's not for you to...

*Marie stands up, letting her piece fall, and grabs the edge
of the table, raising it slightly. Everything on it rolls
around.*

MARIE: *(yelling)* Cut it out, I said! Cut it out!

Gisèle stands up as well. Mimi, Simone and Laurence

151

continue sewing while trying to catch the spools that are rolling around the table. The presser sets down his iron, walks over, and tries to joke around.

THE PRESSER: Go ahead, fight, kill each other, but don't hurt yourselves...

MARIE: Who asked you to butt in?

The presser retreats. The sewing machine operators poke their heads in the door to see what is going on. Gisèle gives up first. She drops her work and runs out, jostling the sewing machine operators. Marie releases the table and drops onto her stool. The sewing machine operators keep watching.

THE SEWING MACHINE OPERATORS: Say, what's going on?

MIMI: *(yelling at them)* Go blow, you creeps! Nothing's going on, nothing. You guys stay out. No men allowed here. We don't go bugging you in your hideout, do we? I can't believe it... *(The sewing machine operators retreat. Suddenly Marie slumps down on the table and bursts into tears. She will recover very soon and start working again.)* Hell, this is real cheery: one of us is bawling in the toilet and one is bawling in here! Shit! *(Madame Laurence shakes her head disapprovingly and whistles through her teeth.)* Stop that, it gets on my nerves!

Madame Laurence continues, ignoring her comment. Silence.

SIMONE: There are days when everything goes wrong, even the thread keeps breaking...

Mimi finishes her piece and doesn't take another. She rummages in her canvas bag and takes out her messkit, then concludes.

MIMI: Damn if this will make me lose my appetite... Nice and hot, on the double...

She extends her messkit to the presser who removes his iron from the gas burner and sets the kit in place.

THE PRESSER: Anyone else?

Madame Laurence brings hers. Marie throws down her piece, stands up and exits, grumbling.

MARIE: I'm eating out.

She has already exited. Laurence, Simone and Mimi note her departure, gesturing to each other.

MIMI: *(concluding)* Boy, that was something...

MADAME LAURENCE: *(to Simone)* Once again, you didn't bring anything warm?

SIMONE: I didn't have time to make anything.

MADAME LAURENCE: You mean you didn't have the energy...

MIMI: Shit, got to eat... Or else...

MADAME LAURENCE: One should eat fatty foods! *(Mimi and Laurence set a makeshift table for themselves at their end. They start working again while their messkits are heating up. Simone has also completed her piece. She takes a small package*

153

out of her bag and, after making herself comfortable, starts nibbling. Madame Laurence addresses Simone.) I'll have you taste some...

MIMI: Is today a good day or a bad day, Madame Laurence?

MADAME LAURENCE: Even when it's a bad day I manage to make it into a good one.

MIMI: No kidding? How?

MADAME LAURENCE: *(explaining while giving some of her food to Simone to taste)* When I make a stew, even if I don't have any meat, I still put in a bit of sage. That way when it simmers, it tastes of leg of lamb.

MIMI: And when you fart?

MADAME LAURENCE: *(sanctimoniously)* Please, we're dining...

> *Gisèle re-enters. She notices Marie's empty stool.*

GISELE: Where'd she go?

MADAME LAURENCE: She's eating out...

GISELE: Well, some people sure pamper themselves...

MIMI: Hey, hey...

> *She gestures to Gisèle to shut up. Gisèle shrugs her shoulders. She takes out her messkit and brings it to the presser.*

THE PRESSER: Two shifts now?

154

Gisèle doesn't answer. She fills up an empty bottle at the faucet behind the pressing table and brings it to the table.

GISELE: We ought to get together and buy some lithia, that way we could have as much bubbly water as we want...

MIMI: Go ahead, buy some, if you have cash to waste...

GISELE: I don't believe in saving money where health is concerned...

They have all settled down to eat. A voice is heard rising from the courtyard. A man is singing "White Roses". They all listen while eating. Madame Laurence has opened the window. Simone, the first to finish eating, stands up and sits by the window. She bends out the window to see the singer. Mimi and Gisèle bustle about.

MIMI: Should we put in buttons?

MADAME LAURENCE: No, come on, the poor man...

MIMI: Let's put in twenty coins and some buttons; it'll be noisier...

Simone is joined by Gisèle, followed by Mimi who throws down the little packet of money and buttons wrapped in a piece of newspaper. The voice stops singing and shouts.

THE VOICE: *(off)* Thank you, ladies and gentlemen.

Simone has settled back to work with a new piece. Mimi takes a five-minute break after the meal. She smokes a cigarette as she watches the others work. She stares in astonishment at Simone who is crying softly.

SCENE 3

NATURAL SELECTION

1946, late afternoon. All the women workers are present. No one is at the pressing table.

SIMONE: Yesterday a guy followed me.

MIMI: No, really? With the look on your face when you're walking alone...

GISELE: Let her have her say.

MIMI: I ran into her the other day. I swear, she scared the wits out of me. A grey mouse on patrol: one-two, one-two...

SIMONE: That's just it. Yesterday, I come out of the Red Cross where I had to drop off a photo...

MARIE: Of yourself?

SIMONE: No, of my husband, which bothers me because I've dropped off so many. I have hardly any left... Anyhow... As usual, I'm running. I get in line. It's my turn. Before you know it, I'm out the door. Then, bingo, I bump into this guy...

MARIE: What was he like?

SIMONE: A guy, nothing special... I apologize. He apologizes. We hem and haw, and I don't know, I must've smiled at him without realizing it.

GISELE: Oh-oh! Never smile... Never... Snap back...

SIMONE: I smiled and it was too late. That was it. I was stuck, couldn't get rid of him. Blah-blah-blah, blah-blah-blah...

MARIE: What'd he say?

SIMONE: How should I know? I don't listen...

MADAME LAURENCE: Was he offensive?

SIMONE: Not really. He went on about my eyes... A lot of silly sweet talk... As a result I didn't dare leave the subway...

MARIE: This was in the street or the subway?

SIMONE: I couldn't *not* take the subway. I had to get home.

GISELE: He followed you into the subway?

MADAME LAURENCE: Some men have nothing better to do with their time.

SIMONE: That's exactly what I said to him: don't you have anything better to do with your time?

GISELE: You talked to him? Oh-oh! Never talk...

SIMONE: Then I got scared... I didn't dare get off at my stop...

MARIE: Were there people in the subway?

SIMONE: Not too many, thank God... Can you imagine...

MIMI: What could he have done to you? Knocked you up through your coat?

SIMONE: Fine for you to joke... I'd like to see you...

GISELE: Pretty unlikely. She's the one who latches on to them and they cut and run afraid to become unwed fathers...

MARIE: Sometimes you meet nice people. I always say the best place is dances. It's not true, the best place is buses... Especially if you take the same one every day. So what happened?

SIMONE: I told a policeman that a guy was...

MIMI: So then the policeman started harassing you?

MADAME LAURENCE: They're not like that...

MIMI: Right... Sorry. Me, I'd be petrified of a cop, not some guy who goes on about my eyes!

MADAME LAURENCE: They're not like that. They help out...

MIMI: Sure, sure...

GISELE: Must be the same as in everything. Some good, some bad...

While Mimi responds.

MIMI: Yakety-yakety-yak.

Laurence nods to Gisèle in approval.

MADAME LAURENCE: Exactly!

158

SIMONE: Those who came in '42 were the helpful types. One insisted on carrying my things to the police station.

GISELE: You were arrested?

SIMONE: They weren't after me, they were after my husband. He wasn't home, so they took me and the kids to the station instead. The eleventh precinct... The police captain, also very nice, looked at my papers and told me to go home. He said they didn't have orders to arrest French citizens...

MADAME LAURENCE: Your husband wasn't French?

Simone shakes her head.

MIMI: Boy, I can imagine, you must've been pissing in your panties.

SIMONE: So I grabbed my things and the two kids... But my older boy didn't want to just pick up and leave. He was fuming: "Who's carrying mom's stuff?" he yelled. "You made us come for nothing". I dragged him by the arm — almost yanked it off — and we ran home...

She laughs; they all laugh.

GISELE: *(wiping her eyes)* Cute, poor thing...

SIMONE: When I got home, one thing was missing: a big pocket watch my husband had from his father that was always lying on the kitchen cabinet.

MIMI: One of the fuzz must've swiped it...

SIMONE: I was surprised because they were the nice type, helpful and all... Not like the ones who came afterwards and took my husband away. They kicked down the door!

MARIE: Why'd they do that?

SIMONE: They knocked, we didn't answer, so... The manager says it's up to me to replace it. I've already had it repaired but you can still see it's been damaged. It's not like a new door... Seems it looks offensive from the stairway... Mind you, he could also repaint the place, it's chipping all over... Anyway...

Silence.

MARIE: And so what about that guy?

SIMONE: What guy?

MARIE: The guy, what was he like?

SIMONE: *(evasive)* A guy...

MARIE: Young?

SIMONE: Nothing special...

MADAME LAURENCE: You should've told him you had children, that you were in a hurry. There's always a way of letting them know...

SIMONE: I did nothing else but. I told him I had two grown children. "I love children," he says!

GISELE: Damn!

160

MADAME LAURENCE: It all depends on the tone of voice...

SIMONE: What's that supposed to mean?

MADAME LAURENCE: *(repeating)* It all depends on the tone of voice.

Brief silence.

SIMONE: I didn't do anything wrong, you know...

MIMI: Let it ride. She's Miss Sourpuss...

MADAME LAURENCE: Strange, it never happens to me! *(Mimi is overcome with laughter.)* Go on, laugh away. They can immediately tell whom they're dealing with...

SIMONE: I kept telling him he was wasting his time! What else could I do?

MADAME LAURENCE: Come, come, no one's blaming you.

SIMONE: She's beginning to get on my nerves...

GISELE: You should never answer, you should snap back, I tell you, snap back...

> *Silence. They are now hard at work, frantically trying to complete their pieces before leaving. Night has fallen. After finishing, each one puts away her piece and her belongings; some of the women count their tickets, then change clothes and exit. Hélène has entered and settled down at her lining table; she starts working as the women workers leave. A heap of unironed clothes lies on the pressing table. When*

the last woman has left, Hélène stops basting momentarily and starts tidying up. She is visibly annoyed. She sorts out the buttons, which were left in a jumble, puts away the spools, folds unfinished jackets, and hangs up garments lying about. Léon enters and glances at the pressing table.

LEON: He never showed up today?

HELENE: Who?

Léon points to the pressing table. Hélène shrugs her shoulders.

LEON: You should tell him to keep regular hours; to come either in the morning or in the afternoon... So we'll know when we can count on him...

HELENE: Tell him yourself.

She is back at her table.

LEON: Why? Why me? *(Silence.)* What's that supposed to mean, tell him yourself?

Silence.

HELENE: *(while working)* If you have things to tell him, you tell him. Period. That's all.

LEON: He doesn't iron well, doesn't work well, I shouldn't have hired him?

Silence.

HELENE: *(with difficulty)* I can't look at him...

LEON: So don't look at him... Talk without looking...
(Pause.) O.K., O.K., fine... I'll tell him, I'll tell him... *(He is
about to exit but walks back and resumes.)* That's awful, just
because he's been deported, he shouldn't work? "I can't
look at him" — what's that supposed to mean? He's no
different from anyone else, is he? *(Hélène doesn't answer.)*
What's wrong with him? What's wrong with him? He's as
strong as a horse; all day he has a ten-pound iron in his
hands; when he's not ironing here, he does the small press
at Weill's and I'm sure he's got a third job in the evening
and a fourth at night... The only thing is, I want him to tell
me when he'll be at Weill's and when he'll be here, that's
all... I should always have workers like him, I can't wish for
better, he's a man of iron, tough as nails, never a
complaint, never a peep, he knows the meaning of work.
Don't worry, the ones who came back from there, they
know... That's what's called natural selection, madam...
*(Hélène says nothing; she has stopped working; she suddenly
exits, wiping her eyes. Léon continues while following her out.)*
Now what? Any time you try and have a serious talk with
her...

He turns off the lights as he exits.

SCENE 4

THE PARTY

1947. Late afternoon. Everyone is working. After checking the time, Marie and Gisèle stand up and start setting things up for the party.

GISELE: *(to those still working)* Enough, enough, time to stop. *(As she starts shoving the table against the wall.)* Clear off, we've got to set things up.

MIMI: Mind letting me finish my piece?

SIMONE: *(standing up)* You'll finish tomorrow.

MIMI: *(still working assiduously)* Just because she talks to any old person in the bus I should lose a piece!

MARIE: *(laughing as she grabs the work from Mimi's hands)* Come on, stop!

MIMI: They're beginning to get my goat. I'm not getting married, am I?

> *Meanwhile Madame Laurence has stood up, removed her smock and put on her coat.*

MARIE: *(while putting on fresh makeup)* What are you doing Madame Laurence?

MADAME LAURENCE: I'm going home, dear.

MARIE: You're not staying for...

MADAME LAURENCE: Unfortunately I can't choose the

people I work with, but when it comes to pleasure... I consider...

MIMI: When it comes to pleasure, I doubt she often gets to choose.

GISELE: *(while combing her hair)* Come, Madame Laurence, everyone here is fond of you.

MADAME LAURENCE: Cock-and-bull! I know what's what.

MARIE: Stay for my sake; it would make me so happy.

MADAME LAURENCE: I wish you a great deal of joy and happiness, dear, but I've finished my work for the day and I have a train to catch.

MIMI: *(also fixing herself up)* Leave her alone. Since Madam is too proud to party with us.

SIMONE: *(she, too, has put on fresh makeup)* Madame Laurence, on occasions like these shouldn't we let bygones be bygones?

GISELE: It sure isn't a day to sulk!

MADAME LAURENCE: As long as some people keep talking behind my back!

She wavers next to the door.

GISELE, SIMONE and MARIE: Come, come! She's imagining things, it's awful!

MIMI: *(to Madame Laurence)* Is that meant for me?

SIMONE: She didn't mention you, come on!

MIMI: Is that meant for me?

MADAME LAURENCE: Whoever feels crummy...

MIMI: Listen, darling, I talk behind your back out of politeness, believe it or not.

MADAME LAURENCE: Well believe it or not, I don't like it. And don't darling me, we're not old cellmates...

MIMI: *(cutting her off)* A cell is where you belong...

GISELE: Come on, come on, shake hands and let's forget about it.

MIMI: Me, shake hands with her? Who do you think I am? I'm an honest woman.

MADAME LAURENCE: Easy to say!

MIMI: O.K., you asked for it. You want to know up front what I think of you from behind?

MADAME LAURENCE: I couldn't give less of a damn, believe it or not. Good evening.

MIMI: *(preventing her from leaving)* Oh, no! Oh, no! You're not going to get off so easy. She fucks things up, screws up our party and expects to make a grand exit?

She pushes her into the center of the workroom.

MADAME LAURENCE: *(backing up, hysterical)* Don't touch me!

SIMONE: Mimi! Madame Laurence!

MIMI: So you want to know what we think? We're fed up with your airs — fed up, do you hear? And another thing you'd better get into your thick skull — you weren't born with this stool up your ass!

MADAME LAURENCE: What in the world is she saying? What's she saying? Let me go...

MIMI: *(continuing)* While we ruin our eyes in artificial light day in and day out, Madam sits next to the window by divine right! I mean really...

MADAME LAURENCE: It's my seat. I see no reason to give it up and I won't.

MIMI: Tomorrow I'll park my fanny there. I can have a crack at making eyes at the concierge too, can't I?

MADAME LAURENCE: What?

> *Léon enters panic-stricken, followed by Hélène who is made up and wearing a party dress.*

LEON: Now what's happening?

MADAME LAURENCE: Monsieur Léon, Monsieur Léon, it's starting up again!

LEON: What is?

MADAME LAURENCE: *(pointing to Mimi)* She wants to take my seat.

MIMI: How come she's glued to the window; why can't we each take turns?

GISELE: One week one person, another week another, it would be fairer, wouldn't it?

MADAME LAURENCE: You see, you see! They're ganging up on me.

LEON: What's the big deal being next to the window? It's full of drafts, isn't it?

MIMI: Right, we're concerned for her health.

GISELE: We want fresh air too.

MIMI: We can't see a darn thing in your crummy workroom, Monsieur Léon. We're ruining our eyes, do you realize what that means? And Madam has a monopoly on the window and the sunlight.

LEON: What sunlight? There's never any sunlight; in five minutes probably it's going to rain...

MIMI: We have to beg her to open the window. Madam is always cold. And when we want it closed, Madam is having one of her days, with hot flashes, damn it!

GISELE: And she gets to look outside and refuses to report on what she sees. I'm sorry, I finally let it out, but tough...

LEON: *(opening the window and looking out)* But there's nothing, nothing to see, it's a courtyard, a courtyard. There's nothing, absolutely nothing!

MIMI: Right, that's what we want to see for ourselves.

LEON: O.K., O.K., fine, I understand. I was told there's a party and we finish sooner because Marie's getting married. I said no problem, why not! I'm not a dog, right? We're civilized. Then what happens? A revolution! So, if that's the way things are, the party's off. Everybody sit down and get back to work.

MIMI: *(cutting him off, yelling louder)* We want better lighting, we don't want to ruin our eyes anymore, and we don't want any more favoritism around here... We've had enough... Enough is enough... And we don't want your rotten stools anymore, we want chairs, so there!

MADAME LAURENCE: *(in an undertone to Léon)* Monsieur Léon, they resent me because my husband's a government employee. That's the real truth, why don't you come out and say it? They're jealous.

GISELE: Yes, Monsieur Léon, chairs!

SIMONE: Who ever mentioned your husband, Madame Laurence, who?

MADAME LAURENCE: Yes, my husband's a government employee; he most certainly is and I'm proud of it!

MIMI: *(singing)* "Marshal Pétain/ Here we are/ You are the savior of France".

MADAME LAURENCE: *(coming toward her with clenched fists)* So what? So what?

> *Brief silence. Mimi turns her back to her, suppressing laughter.*

LEON: O.K., is it over now? Is it over?

MIMI: *(to Gisèle)* Now it isn't behind her back anymore!

MADAME LAURENCE: You said a lot of other things which you wouldn't dare repeat.

MIMI: Want to bet?

LEON: That's enough now, enough!

MARIE: *(on the verge of tears, to the women)* You're mean, for once that I'm getting married.

LEON: Serves you right, that'll teach you to make such a fuss and commotion... So what's the result? An hour wasted, wailing and sobbing...

Madame Laurence is lead away by Hélène and Simone.

HELENE: Stay, you'll make the girl happy.

MADAME LAURENCE: No, no, absolutely not. That I should be insulted... *(She makes a gesture indicating indifference.)* But my husband, no!

SIMONE: No one mentioned your husband, Madame Laurence. We've never set eyes on the man.

MADAME LAURENCE: That would be the last straw. *(In an undertone to Hélène)* He saved some Jewish people, you know, unlike some.

HELENE: Of course, of course.

MADAME LAURENCE: And not for money, like some, not him.

SIMONE: Come, take off your coat. You'll get cold when you go out.

Madame Laurence allows her coat to be removed and continues in a low voice.

MADAME LAURENCE: He even gave some of them advance warning.

HELENE: Who's still thinking about all that, Madame Laurence? Who's still thinking about all that...

MADAME LAURENCE: He took risks, unlike some...

LEON: Hélène , what are the guys up to?

MIMI: Oh no. No men allowed. It's off limits here.

LEON: What about me?

MIMI: You're not a man, you're a monkey. Jack wanna banana?

LEON: Oh! Oh! And what about the presser? He's not a man either?

The presser apologizes for his presence with a gesture.

MIMI: Every harem has to have a eunuch...

The sewing machine operators enter.

THE SEWING MACHINE OPERATORS: So, is this where they're handing out the booze? Who's treating?

LEON: Marie's getting married. So...

HELENE: The small press left; we forgot to tell her...

The sewing machine operators continue while surrounding Marie.

THE SEWING MACHINE OPERATORS: The only sexy one and she's being snapped up... So where's your gigolo, Marie, huh?

Gisèle and Marie take out the bottles as Simone fetches the gift. She waits for silence.

SIMONE: On behalf of all my co-workers...

Marie bursts into tears and kisses Simone.

MARIE: You shouldn't have, you shouldn't have.

SIMONE: *(sobbing as she hugs Marie tightly and repeats)* Be happy, be happy.

MIMI: Oh-oh, here goes the mush. Turn on the music, damn it.

She sings. They all kiss Marie who is crying in front of her unwrapped gift.

MADAME LAURENCE: I too contributed to your gift, dear. All my best wishes.

MARIE: *(kissing her eagerly)* Thank you, thank you.

> *Léon rushes back in, carrying a record player and several records. He puts a record on; it is a Yiddish tango.*

MIMI: What's that?

LEON: A tango. Are you familiar with tangos?

SIMONE: *(explaining to Marie and Gisèle)* No, it isn't German, it's Yiddish.

> *With tears of laughter, Simone translates the tango's extremely vulgar lyrics.*

GISELE: What's Yiddish?

SIMONE: What Jews speak.

GISELE: And you speak it?

SIMONE: Yes.

GISELE: So you're Jewish?

SIMONE: Well, yes.

GISELE: Well, yes, I'm a dope, I know... That's funny.

SIMONE: What's funny?

GISELE: Nothing. I knew Monsieur Léon was, and his wife too. But you... I can't get used to the idea... It's ... It's strange but true, you're... By the way, then maybe you could tell me what was the problem between you and the Germans during the war? *(Simone remains speechless. Gisèle*

173

continues.) I mean... How do you explain that you, the Jews, and they, the Germans... Since... I'm sorry, how should I put it? There are a lot of points in common, aren't there? I was talking about it with my brother-in- law the other day. He was saying, before the war Jews and Germans were like two peas in a pod...

> *Simone doesn't answer. She looks at Gisèle.*

LEON: *(while dancing with Marie, pushes the presser toward Simone)* Do you know how to dance?

THE PRESSER: Me?

LEON: *(thrusting him in Simone's arms)* So, go on, ask her, she only has two children and a three-room apartment.

> *The two couples whirl around; everyone is having fun and toasting. Madame Laurence, wrapped in her coat, her bag on her lap, is seated in a corner. She is holding a glass. Simone appears moved as the presser holds her in his arms. He doesn't talk to her; he is counting the steps. Léon murmurs sweet little nothings into Marie's ear, making her blush and laugh. Mimi is dancing in a very suggestive way, in the popular "musette" style, with a very short sewing machine operator who is sweet-talking her in Polish. She winks at Simone and shows her how to "rub" against her dance partner. The record comes to an end and Léon rushes to turn it over.*

HELENE: *(next to the record-player)* Don't you have anything else?

LEON: What?

HELENE: I don't know. Something more usual.

LEON: I don't see what you mean.

HELENE: Really, it makes a crummy impression.

LEON: What? *(Hélène shrugs her shoulders. Léon controlling himself)* What makes a crummy impression? *(Hélène shrugs her shoulders and walks away. Léon follows her while the next tune begins. It's a waltz, also in Yiddish.)* What makes a crummy impression?

HELENE: Forget it. It makes a great impression, O.K.? I didn't say anything.

LEON: Yes you did! Yes you did!

GISELE: *(kissing Marie)* I have to head home. Soon it will be your turn — a fit if you're ten minutes late.

MADAME LAURENCE: *(standing up, a bit jolly)* I'll leave with you... You'll have to train him dear, train him, or else...

SIMONE: *(to the presser)* Do you want to?

THE PRESSER: It's a dance tune?

SIMONE: It's a waltz.

THE PRESSER: I don't know if...

SIMONE: You just have to turn.

THE PRESSER: Do you like this?

SIMONE: Dancing?

THE PRESSER: No, Yiddish?

MIMI: *(still in the sewing machine operator's arms)* So, the happy couple, any progress?

THE PRESSER: *(clasping Simone)* Do we give it a try?

SIMONE: Let's.

> *The presser takes the plunge, and both of them almost fall. Simone bursts out laughing. In a corner, Léon and Hélène are arguing.*

SCENE 5

NIGHT

1947. The workroom is plunged into semi-darkness. Simone is working in silence. In front of her, there are candles or an oil lamp. The presser is sitting on his pressing table, idle.

SIMONE: I won't be long.

THE PRESSER: *(grumbling)* No one's waiting for me...

Silence.

SIMONE: They still won't give me a death certificate. A lady told me she heard a "missing person" certificate was sufficient. Depends for what... Not for a pension... They're always making us fill out new forms; they don't even know what we're entitled to. No one knows anything. We get shuttled from office to office. *(Pause.)* We've gotten to know each other from standing on the same lines. We talk and exchange information... Oh, there's no end to the tall stories... There are always some know-it-alls... Worst are the mothers... Did you come through the Hotel Lutetia? *(The presser nods.)* I was told to go there, way in the beginning, to get information — someone who might have seen him, who... Well, you know, by showing the photographs, the... I only went once and I didn't dare go up to anyone. There was a woman who grabbed me by the arm and stuck a photograph under my nose — a kind of yearbook picture — I can still see the kid, he was about the age of my eldest, wearing short pants and a tie, and holding a book. "The top student in the class," she was yelling, "he's always the top student in the class." She wouldn't let me go. "Why are you crying?" she asked again and again. "Why are you crying? Look, look, they're coming back. They'll all come back. It's God's will, God's will." Then another woman started screaming and pushing her... Even if they're told there's no hope as far as the children are concerned, they come anyway. They're there, they talk... I saw her again several times in the offices, crazier and crazier each time... Another one, she never wants to stand on line. Madam always has to be ahead of everyone else. Once I said to her: "You know, we're all in the same boat, you don't have to jump the line, there's enough misfortune to go around..." At Police headquarters, I met a Madame Levit, with a "t", very nice this one, very proper. She was really unlucky. Her husband was also taken in '43, but he wasn't even Jewish, can you imagine? His name was Levit, that's all... Since then, she hasn't stopped running around. In the beginning, during the war, it was to prove that he was... *(She searches for the right word.)*

THE PRESSER: *(prompting her)* Innocent?

Simone nods.

SIMONE: And now, like the rest of us, she runs around to find out what became of him and tries to collect a small pension. She's all alone with three children, no profession, no training, nothing to fall back on... *(Silence. The presser looks at her without saying anything. Simone continues.)* The worst is not knowing, thinking that maybe he's lost somewhere and doesn't remember his name, or me, or the children. That happens, you know, but I tell myself that even that can be cured with time... The other day I left the market and I saw a man from behind holding a shopping basket. I don't know why, but for a split second I thought, it's him! With a shopping basket! It was strange because he'd never even pick up bread, he'd never go marketing. He didn't like to... Anyhow, it just shows, sometimes the mind plays tricks... *(Pause.)* After all if they don't want to make out a death certificate at Police headquarters, it must be because they still think there's hope, no? It must be that even they aren't sure of anything. Otherwise they'd be all too happy to fill out the forms and file them away so that everybody's status would be straightened out and that would be that. Here I've finished. *(She hands him the piece. The presser lights the oil lamp on his pressing table and starts ironing.)*

THE PRESSER: *(while ironing)* Recently I was asked to submit my pay slips from before the war. I told them that I'd left with them and so I'd returned without them... After looking at me wide-eyed, the lady told me to get duplicates made... How can you get duplicates made if you don't have the originals? So she advised me to go see my old bosses and ask them for duplicates... I said thank you very much and left... I didn't have the nerve to tell her that all my old bosses had left with me and anyhow they weren't the types to give out pay slips...

> *He taps the jacket's lapels to give it shape and dispel the steam. He seems to be beating the jacket angrily but, in fact, is only doing what's necessary.*

LEON: *(entering, cheerful and excited)* So you're punching away in the dark out here, huh? Ramadier wants to oust the commies from the government and bingo all of France is in the schwartz. Fortunately they left us gas...

THE PRESSER: *(handing the jacket to Léon)* It's done.

> *Spreading his hands open to form a hanger, Léon gently takes the jacket under its shoulders, brings it near the light and turns it around.*

LEON: Another new style: pockets, lapels, sleeves... Well, if it amuses them and brings in orders, I'm... *(He exits, yelling out.)* I'll only be a minute, I just have to send off this so-called new style with the so-called sales rep. I don't like him at all, a... *(He gestures as though he were tightening the knot of a tie.)*

Simone hasn't moved; she is still sitting and staring, absorbed in thought. The presser sits down next to her.

Silence.

THE PRESSER: *(straining)* He left when?

SIMONE: '43.

THE PRESSER: Late '43?

SIMONE: *(shaking her head)* On the "missing person" certificate it says: "Left Drancy in March '43..." *(Pause.)*

THE PRESSER: Do they say for where?

SIMONE: Lublin Maïdanek, destination... *(Silence.)*

THE PRESSER: How old was he?

SIMONE: Thirty-eight. We married late, there's a ten-year age difference between us.

THE PRESSER: What age did he look? *(Simone doesn't understand.)* Did he look older or younger?

SIMONE: *(still not looking at him)* Maybe a bit older when they took him? He was convalescing. He had been a

prisoner of war for a while in Compiègne. There he got
sick. So they released him. When he came back to Paris,
he had identity papers made at the Jewish Union to
legalize his status. Strange. He had lived in France for
years without papers, but all of a sudden he wanted to be
absolutely ligit... At the Jewish Union they gave him a
residence permit. He wasn't French, still Rumanian, I
mean "stateless of Rumanian extraction", is what they
wrote...

THE PRESSER: *(without listening to her)* Did he wear glasses?

SIMONE: Yes, but not all the time.

THE PRESSER: What about his hair? *(Simone looks at him
without understanding. The presser continues.)* Did he have a
full head of hair?

SIMONE: He was balding a bit but it suited him.

Silence.

THE PRESSER: Just tell yourself he never made it to a
camp... *(Brief silence.)* On arrival the survivors of each
transport were separated into two groups... Those who
would go to the camp and the others. We left on foot, the
others, a larger group, got into trucks. At the time we
envied them... *(He stops.)* The trucks took them directly to
the showers... They didn't have time to realize what was
happening, they didn't go to the camp... *(Pause.)* You know
about the showers?

SIMONE: How can you be so sure? *(The presser doesn't
respond.)* Everyone says that he'll still return, that they're
everywhere — in Austria, Poland, Russia — that they're
being nursed and put back on their feet before being sent

home! *(The presser nods his head in silence.)* Thirty-eight isn't old, it really isn't old. That they did what you say to old people, to those who couldn't work, to women, children, right, we know all that, but...

> *She is interrupted by Léon who enters carrying a tray with tea, a bottle of brandy and cookies. Simone stands up and puts her coat on over her smock. She places her hand on the presser's shoulder momentarily and exits. The presser hasn't moved.*

LEON: *(astonished)* That's a hard one to swallow! *(He exits after her, yelling.)* You don't want a drink? Wait, at least don't go home alone, let us take you back. *(He re-enters.)* She's gone, she's nuts, no? What's wrong with her? If she didn't want to stay she should have said so... Ask for extra help these days and... Once you've accepted, be gracious about it, no? I would have made it myself, that wretched piece. Did you get a load of her? Show-off. Did she say anything to you?

THE PRESSER: It's me, I spoke to her.

LEON: Oh, I see! I see... Do you want tea or a glass of... *(He points to the bottle.)*

THE PRESSER: *(without getting up)* I'm going home, too.

LEON: *(serving him)* No, no, I insist, a glass of... huh? *(The presser doesn't react. Léon serves himself.)* You did the right thing, you did the right thing... I've been wanting to talk to her, too, for a long time, but...

THE PRESSER: *(as if to himself)* If only one could cut out one's tongue.

182

LEON: You're right, you're right: "If only one could cut out one's tongue!" *(Suddenly he yells, as though he were suffocating.)* Hélène ! Hélène ! *(To the presser)* What can I say? You have to have resilience in life... *(He points to Simone's seat.)* That's what she's missing. So, naturally, she... *(He searches for his words.)* She...

THE PRESSER: *(standing up)* I'm going home.

LEON: Nothing doing, we'll have a drink. Otherwise... *(He gestures vaguely and spills the two glasses.)*

HELENE: *(entering, all made up, wearing a bathrobe over her nightgown)* Simone left?

LEON: Yes. *(Pointing to the presser, in a low voice)* He spoke to her. *(Hélène looks at the presser without saying anything. Léon lifts his glass and offers the other to the presser who takes it automatically.)* Go on, drink, drink. *(They drink.)* I wanted to talk to her myself, really, really, only... I'm afraid of my words, afraid! I prepare a kind sentence, full of common sense and human understanding and something horrible comes out instead... It's as if I had verbal diarrhea. It's awful, it's always like that ... *(He spits, then to Hélène)* Isn't true? It is, I know what I'm like, I know...

HELENE: Please stop drinking, will you.

LEON: *(indignant)* I didn't drink anything... *(He turns toward Simone's stool and suddenly yells.)* On the shelves of German housewives, in their stock of black soap, that's where he is, that's where you should look for him, not in offices, not on lists, not in files...

HELENE: *(stands and shoves him back into his seat with all her might)* That's enough. Have you gone crazy or what?

The presser hasn't reacted. Léon tries to laugh, pointing at Hélène. He turns to the presser for approval.

LEON: Tut, tut, tut... She never had the slightest sense of humor. Never... What can you do: she's a German Jew. Every nation has the Yids it deserves... *(He laughs.)* The dregs of the dregs of the earth, Madam, that's what you are. *(He pretends to spit on her.)*

HELENE: *(shrugs her shoulders and mutters)* Polak humor! Very refined... *(She yawns.)*

THE PRESSER: *(standing up)* O.K., I'm going home...

LEON: You're in a rush to toss and turn in bed? Stay a bit... You're comfortable here, aren't you? *(He opens the window.)* Look. No light. They'll still be on strike tomorrow. You'll be able to lie in bed all day... Thank you Monsieur Ramadier... Thank you Monsieur Thorez...

THE PRESSER: I can't stay in bed in the morning...

LEON: Why not? There'll be no electricity at Weill's either you know!

THE PRESSER: Habit. I can't stay in bed in the morning anymore.

Silence. The presser pours himself another drink.

LEON: *(going to serve himself)* That's it, that's it, let's drink, let's drink. *(He hums.)* "Drink once, drink twice, joyful companions of Burgundy." *(He sighs then hums his drinking song again.)*

HELENE: *(without moving)* Well, fine, I'm going to bed. *(She remains seated and yawns.)*

LEON: Fine, fine, run to the free zone, go on, go... She left, to join her mother, with the country bumpkins. Not me. I didn't want to. I stayed... Spent the whole war in Paris, yes sir! I even had fake papers and so on. Richard — that was my name — Léon Richard... Yes... I went around everywhere, some days I was me, wearing a star, some days I was Richard, without the star. I even worked a little under that name at a swanky ladies' tailor... An Italian... People used to say to me, "Be careful Monsieur Léon." But I thought, even if I get arrested, what will they do to me? Poke another hole in my ass? No one knew at the time... We were blind... I even used to go to a café to play rummy with some Armenians. And then in late '43, early '44, people everywhere started saying that they were arresting us to burn us, so I began shitting in my pants, and by then it was impossible to get to the free zone which didn't even exist anymore... One day, I get home and the concierge signals to me not to go upstairs. They were up there, three young fellows wearing berets. I saw them come downstairs looking disappointed and exchanging some words with the concierge. He's the one who hid me away in a room upstairs and brought me food and news. I stayed up there, with the blinds closed, like a mole, waiting... And then one day, knock, knock, knock, who's there? "Monsieur Léon, that's it, bad news for the Krauts, they're clearing out." So I exploded, it was fantastic. *(Silence.)* I rushed into the street like a maniac, though I had nowhere to go. I looked at people, their faces. They looked happy, of course. But how should I put it?... *(Pause.)* I went from barricade to barricade... At one point, someone put a rifle in my hands, but they took it right back because they said I was holding it backwards... And then I came upon a crowd next to a truck. A very young guy was getting in, arms raised, hands on his head, pink and blond in his greyish-green uniform, he looked straight at me and, God knows why, I had the feeling this asshole was begging me for help. The men, the Resistance fighters who were making him get into the truck, were roughing him a little so they would look more military, the women were cracking jokes, and he seemed to be calling out to me: "Hey you, yes you, you who knows and has experience, help me, teach me." Suddenly I threw myself at him and yelled: *"Ich bin yude, ich bin yude, ich bin leibedick!"* So he closed his eyes and turned his head away and went way inside the truck to hide... Suddenly all hell broke loose, the women dragged their kids into the buildings. "Another German, in civies, and nasty to boot!" The Resistance fighters surrounded me, the chief aimed his submachine gun at my chest and kept repeating, *"Papir, papir..."* I tried to laugh but my stomach let out a pathetic gurgle, so after catching my breath, I said as calmly as I could, "I'm Jewish, Resistance Officer, sir, I wanted to let him know I'm Jewish and alive, that's all, so I yelled, I'm sorry..." The chief looked at me for a minute without moving — I could clearly see from the expression in his eyes that he still didn't understand why I'd yelled and that he probably never would... I was scared he'd ask me to explain, so I backed away and finally he signaled and the men crowded into the truck. Wonderful! The others kept staring at me, I hung my arms and lowered my head, I couldn't prevent my whole body from crying out in apology, even though I kept telling myself it was over, I was a free man again. It was hopeless... Then I heard the voice of an old-timer from Verdun proclaiming loudly and distinctly, "Here in France, prisoners of war are treated with respect!" The gurgle from my stomach became even more audible. So I made myself invisible, like the invisible

man in the movies, and I left them among themselves —
those people who respected prisoners of war, the Geneva
Convention, Conferences at the Hague, Munich Accords,
Hitler-Stalin Pacts, and crosses, all kinds of crosses — and I
went home. A few days later, the Kraut... *(he points his chin
towards Hélène)* was back and we were cutting our first
mattress out of a kind of felt fabric, half cardboard, half
blotter. People weren't choosy back then, they grabbed
anything they could get their hands on. The happy days,
only you couldn't find fabric or supplies... *(Silence.)* And
you, how did they catch you?

THE PRESSER: *(after a pause)* They caught me!

    Léon nods. Silence.

LEON: *(continuing)* In the beginning I did everything with
Hélène . I cut, pressed, operated the machine, and Hélène
sewed by hand. Then we hired the cop's wife... *(He points to
Madame Laurence's stool.)* Later we came across the nut...
(He points to Mimi's stool.) Then there was a sewing machine
operator who brought over his cousin, and... and so that's
how, with one thing leading to another, as they say, I found
myself up to my neck in this stinking mess.

    Silence.

THE PRESSER: *(stands, yawns and says)* I'm going home.
(He takes a step, then continues.) I won't be coming in
Monday.

LEON: O.K., what do you want me to say? You want your
Monday off? Take it, enjoy. Like the others... What can I
do about it?

THE PRESSER: *(after taking another step)* You'll look for another presser! *(He gathers his belongings and gets ready to go.)*

LEON: What? What's that supposed to mean? Do you want a raise? Is that it? Be honest with me. Don't let it come between us! Not us!

He is on the verge of tears and is holding the presser by the arm.

THE PRESSER: I'll stop by for my pay during the week. Figure out what you owe me. *(He places his box of tickets on the pressing table.)*

LEON: You're crazy! What's the matter? Is someone giving you a hard time? Is it me? Did I say something wrong? Did we piss you off?

THE PRESSER: No, no, it's... *(He doesn't finish his sentence and doesn't gesture.)*

LEON: At least wrap up the week, then we'll see. We aren't savages, are we? We'll discuss it again... We'll work it out... Give me time to sort things out!

THE PRESSER: No...no... It's best like this... Goodbye, Léon. *(He extends his hand.)*

LEON: *(without shaking his hand)* You're not happy here? You're not happy?

THE PRESSER: Yes, I am, I'm fine... So long...

He exits after waving at Hélène who had dozed off during

Léon's narrative and looks on without comprehending.

LEON: *(following him)* I was warned, I was told about this. Never get involved with you people, you're all crazy, all crazy. But you're not the only ones who suffered, damn it, not the only ones! I also had to do despicable things in order to survive... *(He retraces his steps, spills the bottle and the teapot, kicks them and yells.)* Shit!

SCENE 6

THE COMPETITORS

1948. Shortly before noon. The pressing table is unoccupied. Gisèle is standing at the lining table, working. Marie is visibly pregnant.

GISELE: *(while working)* I told her you can do what you like later, when you'll be married, but for the time being I'm still in charge...

MARIE: What did she say?

GISELE: *(shrugging her shoulders)* Nothing, she was already on the landing. I don't even know if she heard me.

MIMI: Bet she did. Count on you to yell and make yourself heard.

GISELE: Look who's talking!

MARIE: You know, at her age it's normal to want to go out... Once you're married...

MADAME LAURENCE: You'd like to go out in your condition?

MARIE: That's not what I meant...

GISELE: "At her age". Believe it or not, when I was her age, I didn't go out...

MIMI: Yea, and look at the result! *(Gisèle looks at her without comprehending.)* Want your daughter to turn out like you?

GISELE: I'm not so bad, there's worse. I'm not complaining...

MADAME LAURENCE: True, you don't look your age...

GISELE: *(hurt)* Thank you very much. *(Silence. Gisèle, to herself)* "Go out," "go out," that's their constant refrain. Personally, I like going home...

MIMI: So you can get into fights with your sweetheart?

GISELE: We don't fight all the time!

MIMI: Hah! I can see it from here: bitchy love! *(She hums a popular waltz.)*

SIMONE: *(to Gisèle)* What about the younger one?

GISELE: Oh, no problem.

MIMI: She isn't itching for it yet...

GISELE: *(to Mimi)* Boy, you can be really disgusting; it's obvious you don't have kids... *(To Simone)* She's doing well in school and... everything's O.K... knock on wood... let's hope it lasts...

MARIE: What would you like your daughters to do later in life?

MIMI: *(to Simone and Marie, twisting her mouth)* Streetwalk, what else!

HELENE: See, I'm not complaining, but I wouldn't want them to end up like me stitching away the whole damned day. Sorry, I'm not going to mince words, it's not a very interesting life... I'd rather they learned to use a sewing machine. It's less exhausting, better paid and more interesting, isn't it?

Mimi hums "Mother stitches and father sews."

MADAME LAURENCE: Sewing machine operator? That's a man's job!

GISELE: In the place where I used to work both men and women operated the machine.

MADAME LAURENCE: *(repeating obstinately)* It's a man's job.

MIMI: Why? Does it take balls to push the pedal?

Madame Laurence utters a pained "oh" while the others burst out laughing.

MADAME LAURENCE: Trying to have a serious conversation with you is so wonderful. In no time you let us know what's on your mind...

MIMI: What, balls? They're no more on my mind than anything else, probably less...

MADAME LAURENCE: *(between her teeth)* Always dirty...

MIMI: They're not dirty, Madame Laurence, just have to rinse them from time to time or, like everything else, they smell... Tell your husband: when he washes his ass he should also soak his thing...

The others are under the table roaring with laughter.

MADAME LAURENCE: *(stopping up her ears)* Please! Stop! I've heard enough! Leave me alone. I'm sorry I said anything. Oh God, God! *(Madame Laurence has put down her work and run toward the door.)*

MIMI: God-say, he'd be qualified to operate the sewing machine too...

> *Madame Laurence exits passing by Léon who enters with a jacket under his arm.*

GISELE: *(who failed to hear Mimi's last remark)* What did she say? What did she say?

> *Simone and Marie are still convulsed with laughter. Mimi is working with a straight face. Gisèle begs her to repeat her last sentence. Léon looks at Simone, Marie and Gisèle who are not working. They are blowing their noses loudly.*

LEON: Are we laughing or crying?

MARIE: We hardly know anymore, Monsieur Léon, we hardly know. *(She moans.)*

GISELE: A mixture of both, actually!

MIMI: *(with a serious air)* It's hard to keep them quiet, I do what I can, but some days... *(She gestures to show she is powerless.)*

LEON: *(unusually calm he waits for Madame Laurence to return and settle back into her seat before starting.)* O.K. ladies, in your opinion, for whom are we working, the living or the dead? *(No response. Léon continues while turning the jacket so it is visible from all angles — it's an unimpressive item.)* If we're working for the dead, I say this garment makes a very good dead person's garment. Only between you and me, a dead person could easily do without garments, couldn't he? He can be dumped in a rag, rolled up in it, and thrown into a hole... You can even skip the rag and the hole. It's been done, hasn't it? But if you're working for living people, you have to anticipate that a living person will inevitably make certain gestures, like moving an arm, sitting down, breathing, getting up, buttoning and unbuttoning. I'm not talking about wartime when a living person, if he wants to go on living, often has to put up both arms and at the same time... No, I'm talking about ordinary movements, in ordinary life, in the ordinary clothing business. Look at this item. Monsieur Max just returned it to me with a piece of paper pinned to the lapel; I'm going to read to you what's on the piece of paper: "This work is for dead people." *(He shows the piece of paper and continues.)* It's written in large letters! Only one customer tried it on... *(Brief silence.)* That the lining in the sleeve — yes, Madame Simone — came apart, O.K. I know, that's not serious. No use crying over it, these things happen. The salesman said so right away — poor quality thread, a loose stitch — all right... Then the buttons fell off one by one when the customer tried to... *(He makes the gesture of buttoning.)* An automatic reflex, so the customer took a look at the buttonholes — yes, Miss Mimi — look at them yourself: handmade buttonholes?

MIMI: Well, what's wrong with them?

LEON: They look like they're shitting and puking simultaneously... That's what's wrong with them... Then he looked up and saw himself in the mirror, and he ripped this thing off his body, ran out of the store and headed straight to the competitors'... Maybe you've already heard about the competitors? You know, all those people who work a lot better and are a lot cheaper because their overhead is a lot lower... When he saw his customer rush out, the store owner sent all the new merchandise back to Monsieur Max — smack in his face — with a piece of paper pinned to this lapel, and then he rushed off to buy his merchandise at the competitors' too. Monsieur Max received the package, examined it and called me; then I examined it and I have to admit, the customer is right: this work is for dead people! *(Silence. Léon continues, still very professorial.)* Now I have to warn you: those of you who wish to continue working for dead people will have to do so elsewhere... From now on, the work produced here will be exclusively for living people and, believe me, these days the living want their money's worth. It's over, the days when you could palm off the worst kind of crap, overcoats with two left sleeves, jackets that button in the back, et cetera, et cetera. Finished! The war's long over; with a bit of luck there'll soon be another one, who knows, things are going so well everywhere... The post-war period's ended, we're back to the pre-war. Everything's back to normal, everything's available now, name the price, they're even talking about abolishing ration coupons, no more restrictions... All I want is professionalism, do you hear? That's all. *(He slips on the jacket. It is too big for him and it hangs pitifully on all sides.)* Look, look "semifinished"! One shoulder's on the first floor and the other's in the basement... Madame Laurence, you should mind your own work, instead of always minding other people's...

GISELE: The color looks good on you.

LEON: The color? And now you're pulling my leg?

GISELE: No, no, Monsieur Léon, I mean it...

Marie breaks out into a nervous giggle.

LEON: *(yelling)* That's it for now, you've had your fun. From now on, each piece will be checked, rechecked and doublechecked; and if the stitches are too large or it's messy, we'll start over again until it's O.K.! A stitch in time saves nine. And you'll find the pay won't be the same. Oh, you've had the good life here, but that's it, it's over, do you hear? Over. I want this place to be like a hard labor camp now, like elsewhere, everywhere, like at the competitors'. I've been a sucker, huh? *(Simone has stood up as discreetly as possible; she has gone over to the pressing table, put down the piece she has just finished, removed her smock and slipped on her coat. She is now nearing the door and signaling to the other women. Léon notices her by door.)* What! Sit down! Sit down this minute! What are you up to? Where do you think you're going? You think you can just march in and out of here on impulse?

SIMONE: I have an errand; since it's almost lunchtime, I thought...

LEON: Around here I decide when it's lunchtime.

SIMONE: I told Madame Hélène I needed time off, it's important.

LEON: I don't give a damn; I'm the one who's in charge here and I'm the one you have to ask!

SIMONE: You weren't around, so I asked your wife.

LEON: *(yelling)* You should've asked me — me — and I say no, so there! Someone who spends half her time on errands or sick leave...

SIMONE: *(protesting)* I took only one sick leave in three years for eight days and I brought work home.

LEON: Baloney! Anyone who can't work properly should stay away and vacate their seat. Jobs here are in demand, I have requests every day; there's work here all year around, no off-seasons, so you either produce or get out! If you want to moan, cry, or run errands, this isn't the place, this isn't a Jewish charitable organization, the O.S.E. or the J.O.I.N.T... I want people to work, to make faultless merchandise which can be delivered and not thrown back in my face... Who's going to have to shoulder the whole line that Max sent back? Me! Me! I don't want to hear any more laughing, screaming, crying or singing! Starting today no one will be allowed an hour off, do you hear? Not even if your children are in agony, your old folks rotting, or your husbands exploding. I don't give a damn. Understand? Errands, you can run on Saturday afternoons and Sundays.

SIMONE: *(blurting out, on the verge of tears)* But offices are closed!

MIMI: *(to Simone)* Why argue with him, stupid? What are you waiting for? Go out, don't be scared. I'll tell you the ending...

> Simone looks at Léon who looks away. Simone exits. Léon takes Simone's seat and sits there momentarily without talking, exhausted. The women start working again in silence.

LEON: *(to Mimi)* You sure run off at the mouth, don't you?

MIMI: I do all right, thank you...

Silence.

LEON: So tell me, loudmouth, what'll she gain by ruining her health running from office to office...

MIMI: She's entitled to a pension, isn't she, a woman alone with two children!

LEON: Her pension is here, right here! *(He bangs on the table.)* She puts in one hour of overtime every evening, stops running errands all day, and that's her pension, no?

GISELE: She can't stay any later in the evening.

LEON: Why? Who'll be disturbed? The place is open. I stay, don't I?

MIMI: Yes, but at home, all you have to do is stick your legs under the table. Your grub is ready. She has to buy food and cook for the kids.

LEON: *(nodding)* Where there's a will there's a way. What's to her advantage? That's the question. Why would she be entitled to a pension?

GISELE: Her husband was deported, wasn't he?

LEON: But he wasn't even French, Madam, he wasn't French. She's entitled to zilch! Zilch! Pensions are given to the French, not to stateless persons of Rumanian extraction. Who's going to cough up for him, huh? Who? The French? What for? The Rumanians? They never heard of him, he left Rumania when he was twelve, why should they give a damn? The stateless? They're not up to giving; all the stateless left with him and those who came back are all nutcases, like the former presser — remember him?

Anyway, who's still concerned with all that? New camps are springing up; before they even have time to pay for the old ones there are new ones to worry about.

MIMI: She's consulting a lawyer, he'll tell her.

LEON: Sure, sure, a lawyer... He'll tell her...

He gestures as if to say, "to whom am I talking?" He stands up, picks the jacket up off the floor, hesitates, rolls it into a ball, throws it under the pressing table and exits. The women work without looking at each other. Mimi talks without looking up from her work.

MIMI: There's nothing wrong with the work. It's the way he cuts, he cuts any old way... Is it the fault of my buttonholes if it falls badly, if the sleeves bunch up? Go and find buttonholes like these... Let them hold a contest, I'm sure I'd be voted buttonhole champion of the world... Look, look, I'm not kidding, you'd think this buttonhole had a life of its own, it's just missing the gift of speech. And I did it without buttonhole twist, with rotten thread that breaks and gets into knots... Really... Some days... I work but, really, I wonder why... Probably because it's in fashion... I get bawled out and... I have nothing... Nothing... No stockings... No slip... No soap... Nothing... To begin with, I want chocolate, yes, I want chocolate!

GISELE: Why, Mimi, what's gotten into you?

MARIE: You have cravings?

MIMI: Well? Aren't I right? The end of restrictions? For them, yes; and for us, what's in it for us? For us? We don't even have toilet paper to wipe our ass, not even toilet paper... *(Hélène has entered a few minutes ago; Madame*

Laurence and Gisèle try to warn Mimi by coughing, but after noticing Hélène 's presence, Mimi continues immediately.) What? I'm not ashamed, I can say so directly to Madame Hélène , it's the cut that's no good, the cut, not my buttonholes...

Hélène   continues to hang jackets up on the top rod, possibly the jackets Max has returned.

SCENE 7

THE DEATH CERTIFICATE

1949. Afternoon... Mimi, Gisèle, Madame Laurence and Jean, the new presser, are all working; Hélène is at her lining table. Simone is removing her coat and putting on her smock.

HELENE: *(to Simone)* Do you have it? *(Simone nods.)* Show it to me. *(Simone takes a sheet of paper out of a large envelope and carefully hands it to Hélène. Simone takes her seat and starts working. Hélène reads in a low voice.)* "Certificate of Death... The Civil Court of the Seine District hereby declares Monsieur... deceased in Drancy, Seine District." Deceased in Drancy? Why'd they put deceased in Drancy?

SIMONE: *(without raising her eyes from her work)* That's how they do it!

HELENE: *(unable to keep her voice down)* What do you mean, that's how they do it? *(Simone doesn't answer, she is sewing very energetically. Hélène reads on to the end.)* "Deceased in Drancy, Seine District, March 3rd, 1943". What's that supposed to mean? Did he trip on the sidewalk in Drancy, Seine District, and die?

> *The presser walks over, takes the death certificate and reads it. Hélène tries to control herself. Simone works, indifferent.*

JEAN: *(after reading, explains)* They put the last place where the deceased leaves a... legal trace. This is the date and place of his departure for... It's so it'll be... more... *(He searches for the right words.)* more... legal.

HELENE: *(cutting him off)* The date of his departure to where? To where? They don't say it's a date of departure... They say deceased in Drancy, Seine District, period, that's all. *(Jean returns to his pressing table without saying anything. Silence. Hélène walks up and down the workroom, then goes up to Simone.)* On your "missing person" certificate it said he left Drancy on March 3rd, 1943, destination Lublin-Maïdanek. I'm not making that up, am I? Why didn't they put that down? That's all they had to do.

SIMONE: *(after a pause)* You can't put a destination on a death certificate...

HELENE: Why not?

SIMONE: You have to be more precise.

HELENE: Why? *(Simone doesn't reply; she is working more and more frantically. Silence. Hélène suddenly yells.)* You should've refused! You should've refused! You're not required to accept this, on top of everything else!

LEON: *(entering, scissors in hand)* What's going on? What's wrong now? What did she do?

HELENE: *(handing him the certificate)* Here, read this!

LEON: What is it?

HELENE: Read it.

Léon skims the sheet and returns it to Hélène .

LEON: Fine... Fine. Now she won't have to run around from office to office, maybe she'll stay put from time to time.

HELENE: *(handing him back the sheet)* Read it all the way to the end!

LEON: I read it, I read all the way to the end, it's fine, fine, it's properly stamped and everything, it's perfect!

HELENE: Nothing shocks you?

LEON: Shocks *me*? You think it's the first death certificate I've seen? *(He snickers and shakes his head.)* I should only have as many orders this winter...

HELENE: *(yelling)* Deceased in Drancy! Deceased in Drancy!

LEON: So what? Drancy or elsewhere... It's a certificate, isn't it?

HELENE: You dope, "Drancy or elsewhere"! If it's not acknowledged on their forms, with all the stamps and official signatures... Look: Civil Court of the Seine District... Court clerk... Judge... Date of registration... Date of certification... In that case, no one went there, no one got into their boxcars, no one was burned; if they simply died in Drancy or Compiègne, or Pithiviers, who'll remember them? Who'll remember them?

LEON: *(in a low voice)* We'll remember, we'll remember, we don't need a piece of paper, and we certainly don't need to yell.

HELENE: Why do they lie, why? Why don't they just put down the truth? Why not put "thrown live into the flames"? Why not?

LEON: A piece of paper, it's a piece of paper. She needs this piece of paper to try to get a pension, that's all. And she's probably not even entitled to this pension, in fact, she's surely not entitled, but she wants to try, she still wants to run around from office to office, she can't help it, she enjoys filling out forms and filing papers, it's her special quirk and the only purpose of this piece of paper, the only purpose... It's a piece of paper that lets you acquire other pieces of paper, that's all!

HELENE: And how will her children know? They'll see "deceased in Drancy" and that's it?

LEON: They'll know, they'll know; they'll know all too well.

HELENE: Of course, for you, the less one knows the better.

LEON: Those who should know will never know; as for us, we know all too much, all too well...

HELENE: Who should know according to you?

LEON: *(after a moment of silence, between clenched teeth)* The others.

HELENE: What others?

LEON: Don't you yell like that, this is a workroom, people are working here — working, not philosophizing... *(To Simone)* And you, put it away... You don't have to flash your papers at us, we don't hand out pensions, this is a workplace, period, that's all... No need to show off your certificates!

HELENE: Stop screaming at her, I asked to see it.

LEON: And who are you? A judge, attorney, lawyer, Minister for Veterans and War Victims? You want to solve everything by blabbering, huh? Solve my problems first, then if you have time left over, you can take care of other people's problems...

HELENE: What problems do you have?

LEON: Me? None! I'm happy, deliriously happy, so happy I could die. What problems? What problems do I have? And who'll remember me, Madam, huh... Who do you think will remember me, who? *(Hélène exits. Léon sighs then starts feverishly tidying up the workroom; everyone is working in silence. Léon remains standing in the center, arms dangling; no one speaks, no one exchanges a glance. To Simone)* Everything O.K.?

SIMONE: *(shrugs her shoulders as though none of this concerned her)* Everything's O.K.

LEON: Fine... Fine. *(He exits.)*

SCENE 8

THE MEETING

1950. Everyone is hard at work.

LEON: *(to the presser, as he unhooks jackets hanging in the rear of the room over the pressing table)* Can you stay late tonight?

JEAN: I'm leaving at six-thirty...

LEON: Six-thirty, you're an office worker now?

JEAN: Today's Friday, isn't it?

LEON: Yes, Friday, the day before Saturday.

JEAN: Fridays, I leave at six-thirty. For my meeting.

LEON: You have meetings Friday evening and I have to deliver Saturday morning! *(Jean doesn't respond, he is working quietly. Léon shrugs his shoulders and heads toward the door. Just as he is about to exit, he changes his mind and continues talking.)* Is the revolution for tonight, at tonight's meeting?

JEAN: I don't think so.

LEON: *(sighing)* Too bad! It would have been a good excuse for a late delivery tomorrow morning... Too bad... So it's a meeting for deliberating and planning, right? They can't deliberate without you for once?

JEAN: No!

LEON: You're such a bigwig they can't deliberate without you?

JEAN: *(setting the iron down abruptly)* If you're looking for a presser who'll work around the clock for your personal satisfaction...

LEON: Nobody here works for my personal satisfaction...

JEAN: You and me aren't married! There are plenty of other jobs around...

LEON: *(turning to the women for support)* It's like a disease — all the pressers here want out! Is there something wrong with the pressing table? Is it lopsided? Is the iron too heavy? Should I be serving five o'clock tea? Am I an unfriendly monkey? Don't I smile often enough?

> *He makes an awful grimace; the women protest and offer him bananas.*

JEAN: On Fridays — every Friday — I have a meeting and I leave at six-thirty.

LEON: Go, go, leave, leave, God be with you! You know what, we'll split up the work. You have your meetings and attend to mankind's happiness, and I'll stay here and iron all night for tomorrow's delivery — how's that? Does that make you happy? Only there's one thing I'd like to point out. No offence meant. Me — meeting, revolution, or whatever — I have to deliver every Saturday, and I deliver. But you guys, you've been meeting for years and years to talk about change and happiness and try as I might, I see nothing comes from all this talk. Where's the happiness, where's the change?

JEAN: You don't know where to look.

LEON: Show me where to look so I can finally see

something worthwhile for once in my life. Or give me a delivery date. Change on such and such a day; justice, happiness, et cetera, thirty days later.

JEAN: Monsieur Léon...

LEON: "Monsieur", oh dear...

JEAN: That every Friday I go to this meeting and you can't do anything about it, is already a source of great happiness to me and a bit of a change for you, isn't it?

LEON: Granted! Well, then don't forget to tell them I buy the *Farmer and Worker's Almanac* from you every year, and tickets to the *Humanité* festival that I've never attended because it always rains...

JEAN: Don't worry, I'll see to it you're among the last to be executed!

LEON: And my wife too?

JEAN: Your wife too.

LEON: Thank you. It feels good being protected. Simone, you don't have a meeting, so stay. I need you to sew on the buttons. *(He exits without waiting for a reply.)*

MIMI: *(to Simone)* You're a dope, why should you stay? Why don't you tell him to go blow?

GISELE: Can't he ask his wife?

MIMI: Come on, she might chip her nailpolish.

Simone keeps sewing, indifferent.

GISELE: What about your kids?

SIMONE: On Friday evenings, if they don't find me at home, they come pick me up.

MIMI: Well then everything's fine and dandy, if that's the way you want it...

JEAN: You could piss on her head and she'd say thank you... You have rights. You're not even aware of them. How do you expect to get respect?

> *Silence. Everyone is working. Suddenly Simone drops down on the table with her head in her hands and starts sobbing. Everything stops.*

MIMI: Here we go again...

MARIE: Come, what's wrong Simone?

GISELE: *(taking her by the shoulders)* He wasn't trying to be mean...

MADAME LAURENCE: *(to the presser)* You see, you see, why don't you mind your own business? "Rights"!

JEAN: What? I didn't say anything...

MADAME LAURENCE: Oh, sure, go on, we're not deaf.

SIMONE: *(cries and shakes her head)* That's not it...

MIMI: Well, what's wrong? Why are you crying this time? Huh? Want me to tell the monkey you're not staying late, it's no skin off my back.

Simone shakes her head.

MADAME LAURENCE: *(standing up)* Come take my seat. It'll be a nice change for you and you'll have a bit more air. Incredibly hot today and with these winter fabrics...

Simone thanks her with her hand but doesn't move.

MIMI: *(in a low voice)* Are you having your period? *(Simone shakes her head. In an even lower voice)* Were you thinking about your...?

SIMONE: *(still shaking her head)* I wasn't thinking about anything, there's nothing wrong, nothing...

MIMI: Why the hell do you need their pension? Life's fine without it... No sense making yourself sick... Let them keep their lousy pension. They can stuff it! *(Simone shrugs her shoulders indicating "that's not it either".)*

GISELE: It's your kids, they fought again, huh... I can tell you, when the kids annoy *me* I'd rather they cried than me... Last night, I got home and the big one had stained her blouse, a blouse she'd just put on, ready to be washed all over again... "Slob," I said, "you can wash it yourself this time"... But then of course her father sided with her so we yelled and yelled and I cried all night... Couldn't sleep a wink... Oh, I tell you, some days...

Gisèle starts sniffling as well.

MIMI: *(between clenched teeth and threatening Gisèle with her finger)* You, shut up. O.K.?

GISELE: *(pulling herself together)* Now what? I don't have the right to talk?

She starts sobbing, pretending to blow her nose.

SIMONE: *(banging on the table)* Why am I crying? Why am I crying? I don't know...

MIMI: Good, so stop crying and start laughing!

SIMONE: I can't, I can't.

MIMI: Tickle yourself under the arms! *(Simone is still sobbing. Silence.)* O.K., keep crying, kid, you'll pee less! *(Simone laughs between her tears.)* There, you see, that's more like it... Want me to tell you about the hunchback's dick? It was all twisted and crumpled, you had to finger it to make it straight...

Simone shakes her head and her sobbing intensifies.

JEAN: *(while dressing)* Come on, leave her alone, you're driving her crazy with your crap.

MIMI: Mind your own beeswax, O.K....

JEAN: If you all got together and demanded to be paid by the hour, he'd think twice about keeping you late. You have to know how to get respect. Otherwise...

GISELE: Personally, I prefer piece work...

JEAN: By the hour, you do your hours and then you get paid overtime.

GISELE: I wouldn't feel as free...

MIMI: I'm sure you wouldn't, since you pee every five minutes...

GISELE: I pee every five minutes?

MADAME LAURENCE: There's no reason to be ashamed... Come...

GISELE: There's no reason to be ashamed except I don't, that's all...

MADAME LAURENCE: No one's blaming you...

GISELE: I don't, I never...

MIMI: So why do you leave the room?

GISELE: I don't leave the room, the others do...

MADAME LAURENCE: It's awful, you'd think you were being accused of...

JEAN: *(after a brief silence)* Your heads are full of mush.

MIMI: *(showing him the time)* Cut and run pinko or else you'll be late clocking in. *(The presser exits slamming the door. To Simone who is working but still crying)* Now we're among ourselves, you can let it all out.

Simone sobs.

MARIE: She'll choke if this keeps up.

GISELE: You want to lie down on the pressing table?

hiccups) I'll be all right, I'll be all right, I'll be all right...

Brief silence.

MIMI: *(to Simone)* Want to know what I think?

GISELE: Leave her alone.

MIMI: A good screw from time to time would do you a world of good and chase away the blues.

GISELE: Yuk... Big deal... She doesn't have enough troubles as it is? A fellow would mean extra laundry, period, that's all. She already spends half the night scrubbing her kids' laundry.

MIMI: What are professional laundresses for? The birds?

GISELE: Anyhow that's the last thing she needs.

MIMI: *(to Simone)* Don't you listen to her... Look, Sunday I'll take you dancing, you'll pick up some handsome cutie.

GISELE: You're disgusting... Really... Some days...

MARIE: What she needs is someone who'll help her, that she can lean on...

MIMI: "Pete the pimp, he's tall and lean and king of the sidewalk..."

MARIE: *(annoyed, cutting her off)* No I mean something lasting.

MIMI: You've got a point there, the longer it lasts the better

MIMI: You've got a point there, the longer it lasts the better it is... Quickies are not so hot...

They all cave in laughing.

MADAME LAURENCE: *(to Simone, without laughing)* You feel better!

SIMONE: *(wiping her eyes and laughing now)* I don't know what got into me. I was fine, then suddenly I felt like I was suffocating...

MIMI: *(crying from laughter)* Well, yes, after a while you suffocate.

GISELE: Oh, shut up, let her talk... Sometimes I also feel like... feel like... but it doesn't come out, there's like a... like... *(She searches for her words.)*

MIMI: Like what, stupid?

GISELE: Like cotton, right here. *(She taps her chest. To Simone)* Isn't that true, isn't that true? Like a patch of cotton that...?

Simone shrugs her shoulders as a sign of ignorance.

MIMI: *(to Gisèle)* Yeah, but you have no reason, you're happy, you've got a little husband, a little house, little girls...

GISELE: Of course, of course...

SIMONE: Well, me too, me too. The kids are fine. They're doing well at school, there's work here all year around. No off- seasons...

MIMI: You're missing...

GISELE: Leave her alone.

MIMI: Come dance with me on Sunday, I'll tell my Mickey I'm going to see my mother. She gives him the creeps.

SIMONE: Don't be silly, what would I do about the children?

MIMI: You're stuck with them on Sundays too? Well, pal, get smart. Send them out to play football... Or camping...

GISELE: Thanks... So they'll catch cold... Thanks...

SIMONE: Sunday's their day, we go to the movies...

MIMI: Every Sunday?

SIMONE: Except when it's nice out, then we walk around... In the late afternoon we go see my father...

MARIE: Your folks? *(Simone nods.)* With the children?

SIMONE: Have to, no?

MIMI: Well, lovely day I must say... No wonder you... When do you ever take your mind off things?

Brief silence.

SIMONE: Here, with you...

SCENE 9

A NEW LIFE

1951. A summer evening. The windows are wide open. Simone is sitting in Madame Laurence's seat sewing buttons. Hélène is at her lining table, placing garments in cartons and trying to avoid wrinkling them. She becomes agitated.

HELENE: They'll look like rags...

SIMONE: Where are they going?

HELENE: Belgium... *(Léon enters and sits at the table by Simone; he laughs for no reason.)* That's it? It's over?

LEON: Guess what my deal was?

HELENE: What are you talking about?

LEON: I get a hand with three aces, a black king and a red queen. I ask for two cards, put down the king and the queen, and guess what my deal was?

HELENE: Two aces?

LEON: Two aces? One ace! There are only four aces to a deck and I already had three...

HELENE: What do I know? Why isn't Max handling this shipment?

LEON: Do you play cards?

SIMONE: Beggar-my-neighbor with my kids...

LEON: Four aces the first time in my life and wouldn't you know, with my own guys... That's it. From now on if they want to play it'll be for real. We're too old to be playing with buttons. And they're *my* buttons, some gamble for them...

HELENE: Oh! I'm fed up! I can't do this, the cartons are too small!

LEON: Forget it, I'll do it. I always end up doing everything around here...

HELENE: Right, right... Why isn't Max handling this?

LEON: Can't I have my own clients without going through Monsieur Max? I'm not wedded to Monsieur Max for life...

HELENE: Are you sure they'll pay?

LEON: Why wouldn't they pay?

HELENE: Just asking, that's all...

LEON: Just because I've had a few unpaid orders you... *(He stands up and helps Hélène make the package. Simone has finished her piece; she hangs it up and takes another one. Léon to Simone)* Any news of the children?

SIMONE: Yes, a card.

LEON: They're O.K.?

SIMONE: Yes, thank you...

LEON: Where'd they go again?

SIMONE: G.D.R.

HELENE: So, are you helping or yacking?

LEON: I'm helping and yacking, I can do both at once, I don't have two left hands like you...

HELENE: *(watching him momentarily)* Sure, the way you're doing it, it's a cinch, but you don't realize they'll look like rags when they get there... Why don't you roll them up into little balls while you're at it...

LEON: They don't know how to iron in Belgium?

HELENE: O.K., O.K., stop, you're making things worse, I'd rather do it by myself...

LEON: *(to Simone)* G.D.R.? Isn't that Germany?

HELENE: The air's good over there.

LEON: Yeah, yeah, so they say...

SIMONE: They're very happy.

LEON: Did you at least warn them?

HELENE: Léon please.

LEON: What, did I say anything?

HELENE: That's just it, don't.

LEON: It's awful, she knows ahead of time... Anyway...

SIMONE: *(to Hélène)* I didn't want to send them there and then I said to myself, after all, it's being organized by the Federation...

HELENE: You did well, it's a very healthy climate...

LEON: Yeah, yeah...

SIMONE: The older one wrote me they were taken on a bus trip to see Ravensbrück...

LEON: *(to Hélène, suddenly)* Why are you making this package now? You want it to stay wrinkled all night?

HELENE: You told me it had to be shipped first thing in the morning... I made Simone stay on purpose.

> *Simone has hung up the piece she just completed and is getting ready to leave.*

LEON: We'll do it tomorrow, leave it...

HELENE: We won't have time tomorrow!

LEON: I said leave it.

HELENE: No, now that I've started, I'm finishing!

LEON: *(to Simone)* Stubborn, isn't she? You're going to bed now?

SIMONE: Yes, well, I'm going home...

LEON: Shouldn't you be taking advantage of the kids being away on vacation to...

HELENE: Léon!

LEON: Now what?

HELENE: Will you stop?

LEON: What did I say? She's of age... Does she have to be handled with kid gloves like a young girl?

Simone smiles.

SIMONE: You know, evenings I always have things to do around the house and... and... *(She laughs.)*

HELENE: Of course... Of course... They have no idea...

LEON: Who has no idea around here? You're the ones who have no idea... If you don't take advantage of the kids being away to go out and meet people, how do you expect to make a new life for yourself, huh? How?

SIMONE: I have no desire to, Monsieur Léon, I'm fine the way I am... Fine...

LEON: *(in a commanding tone, to Simone)* Sit down... *(He sits down next to her.)* Do you know the Thermometer on Place de la République? It's a café at the corner of the Boulevard Voltaire and Avenue de la République. A large café. Every Sunday morning, there's a woman, Madame Fanny, a very nice woman, who helps people who've... make a new life for themselves. Tell her I sent you, talk to her, and if she has someone who fits the bill — after all, who knows? — she'll introduce you... It doesn't commit you to anything — if it clicks, fine, if it doesn't, you say "thank you, goodbye". There's no entrance fee, no obligation, no strings attached... See what I mean? *(Silence. Hélène looks at Simone. Suddenly, Simone bursts out laughing. Léon to Hélène)* What's wrong? Did I say something funny? Why remain single when you could still make someone happy? There are so many men around who've suffered and are lonely... She's normal, isn't she, so why not live a normal life? And even if she were ugly as sin, with a three-room apartment, she could always find somebody who'd be interested... *(Simone laughs more and more heartily.)* O.K., forget I said anything...

SIMONE: *(calming down)* I'm sorry, Monsieur Léon, I've never gone to the Thermometer café but I was introduced to someone not long ago...

LEON: Ha! Ha! You see? You see!

Simone smiles again.

SIMONE: He even came to the house!

Hélène stops making her package and runs over to sit by Simone as well.

HELENE: Well, that's wonderful! Wonderful!

SIMONE: The kids made things so unpleasant for him that he left and I never saw him again, they were really obnoxious with him... *(She laughs.)* Fortunately, because the person who introduced us later found out he had already remarried thanks to your Madame Fanny. But he didn't find his new wife's accommodations good enough. He was looking for a larger apartment, that's why he asked if he could see mine... *(She laughs.)* You know what he said on his way out? "It's a three-room apartment, but a small three-room apartment..." I have no regrets. I had no desire, and I think that even if I did, I wouldn't be able to...

LEON: You might think that but... They're not all bastards, there are some nice men looking for someone...

SIMONE: The children are too old, they would be miserable, they're used to being the men in the house. And you know, when I married my husband, it was already an arranged marriage, we were introduced... I must say I was lucky, I had no complaints, he was a good husband, but now... it would have to happen differently. Otherwise, I don't think I'd be able... When this guy came to the house — I'd already seen him once before at the house of the person who introduced us — well, when he came to the house...

HELENE: What was he like?

SIMONE: All right, his face was a bit lopsided, but he wasn't too bad-looking. He'd had a lot of misfortunes, a lot of misfortunes... I had trouble containing my laughter in front of him... As soon as his back was turned the three of us cracked up, the younger one imitated him, he re-enacted the whole apartment visit and all his comments... The guy had a little bit of a Jewish accent, which the little one imitates so well, we laughed and laughed... No, it's too complicated, besides, you know, I'm fine the way I am, I've got my freedom, I'd no longer be able to... Anyway... Have a good evening... *(She exits.)*

HELENE: You too. See you tomorrow.

Silence.

LEON: I was only trying to...

HELENE: The things you come up with, really...

Silence.

LEON: O.K., let's go to bed.

HELENE: *(pointing to the unmade package)* You'll do it tomorrow?

LEON: I'll do it tomorrow.

HELENE: We need a larger carton...

LEON: No, no, it's fine.

HELENE: What about the letter?

LEON: What letter?

HELENE: You know...

LEON: We'll write it tomorrow...

HELENE: Tomorrow you'll put it off and the next day you'll put it off again...

LEON: I have no paper.

HELENE: Write it on this and I'll copy it...

LEON: Do you have a pencil?

> *Hélène gives him a pencil.*

LEON: *(reflects momentarily, then)* What should I say?

HELENE: Come on, please, we've been through this a hundred times...

LEON: How should I begin? How do they begin?

HELENE: "Dear cousins".

LEON: "Dear cousins and cousins-in-law".

HELENE: If you like...

LEON: "Dear cousins, second cousins and cousins-in-law".

HELENE: I'll take care of that part.

LEON: Do you want to write the letter?

HELENE: No, it's your cousin, you write it...

LEON: My cousin. He's not even a real cousin, he's a distant cousin and I don't even know her. I never met her. In fact I only saw him twice in my life, at most, when I was a kid. I don't even remember what he looks like, so... *(Hélène sighs without replying.)* O.K.! "Dear distant cousins..." *(He writes.)* Distant cousins. There! Now what?

HELENE: *(dictating)* "If you're still eager to come..."

LEON: Tut, tut, tut... Not so fast... Don't you think we should warn them that things are difficult here too, very difficult, that you have to work hard — hell I don't know, what kinds of expectations do they have, why are they leaving?

224

HELENE: Let's not go over that again, they're leaving because they can't stand it over there anymore...

LEON: *(nodding)* They can't stand it anymore... And is that a valid reason for leaving everything and turning up in a country and at the house of people they hardly know?

HELENE: You don't want them to come? Fine. Just write that you can't have them over, period, that's all, but please stop driving me crazy, we've already discussed this a hundred times!

LEON: I'm asking if we shouldn't warn them, that's all, that things will be difficult here, that you have to work hard, that they shouldn't kid themselves...

HELENE: Who's kidding themselves?

LEON: I don't know, maybe they think around here the streets are paved with gold?

HELENE: *(standing up)* Write whatever you like, I'm going to bed.

LEON: This is awful: you're the one who tells me to write and when I start writing you go to bed.

HELENE: O.K., write: "Dear cousins, you are welcome to come. We're expecting you. See you soon. Signed Hélène and Léon."

LEON: To write that, you don't need me.

HELEN: I want you to write it!

LEON: Why?

HELENE: Because I know you...

LEON: *(sighing)* O.K. "Dear distant cousins. Come. We're expecting you..." No... "If you're still eager to come, write and tell us when you expect to arrive so we can get organized as best we can to put you up when you first get here..." There, is that O.K.? *(Hélène doesn't reply.)* You don't like "when you first get here"?

HELENE: It's easy, if you don't want them to come, write, "don't come"... I've a headache...

LEON: I could write "don't come" to my own cousin who's asking me for help after all the suffering they've been through? I only wanted to... It's our responsibility, isn't it? Do I know what they have in mind, why they want to leave Poland, why they want to come here — here specifically — why they don't go — I don't know — to Israel, for example? Maybe they assume we have a huge factory and that we're rolling in gold and diamonds.

HELENE: *(furious)* They're communists, they don't give a damn about gold and diamonds, they have no family in Israel, their children speak French, they want to come to France, to live in France, to work in France!

LEON: If they're communists why don't they stay over there where they're all communists?

HELENE: O.K., I'm going to bed.

LEON: So we can't even talk anymore? I'm trying to...

HELENE: *(cutting him off)* Talk to the walls, I'm exhausted, I've a headache. It's your family, do what you want, write what you like...

Léon nods. Hélène exits, crying.

LEON: This is awful, what did I say, what did I say? Is it my fault, my fault, my fault, if it's a stinking mess everywhere?

SCENE 10

MAX

1952. Late afternoon. Everyone is hard at work, except Simone who is not present. Mimi is humming. Léon enters in a panic, running like a pursued man, and makes a beeline for the pressing table; he hides under it, behind a pile of unironed jackets. Hélène's voice can be heard from the corridor:

HELENE: *(off)* But I tell you he isn't here.

MAX: *(off)* So where is he? Where is he?

HELENE: *(off)* How should I know, we're not stitched to each other...

MAX: *(off)* I want my merchandise, do you hear? I want my merchandise, I won't leave without it.

HELENE: *(off)* As soon as it's ready...

MAX: I know, I know, you'll put it all into a taxi... *(Max has entered followed by Hélène who tries to calm him; Max is visibly in a state of nerves; he gazes at the workroom for an instant, distraught, and discovers the pile of finishing work awaiting Simone on her stool; he groans.)* But nothing's ready, nothing...

HELENE: *(smiling)* Come now, Monsieur Max, everything that was ready was already delivered to you.

MAX: *(yelling while picking garments from the floor or grabbing them out of the women's hands)* Size forty, only size forty. I

228

need every size and all you delivered was size forty. Size forty's useless to me... *(He continues picking up garments and putting them down further away. He moves the pile under the pressing table and discovers Léon.)* Léon!

LEON: *(as though he were waking up)* Eh? What?

MAX: So you've taken to hiding under tables!

LEON: Me? Hiding?

MAX: How come I haven't received...

LEON: *(pursuing his train of thought)* Who's hiding? Why would I hide in my own place? I've done enough hiding in my life, thank you... Incredible... So now I'm not allowed to go and come as I please under my own pressing table?

MAX: *(controlling himself)* Léon, Léon. Why'd you tell me on the phone this morning you'd put the rest of my merchandise into a taxi and it would get to me any minute?

LEON: *(yelling)* Me? I said that? I said something over the phone? Do I even have time to answer the phone?

MAX: No, not you, your wife.

LEON: *(aggrieved)* Hélène, why do you say such things? *(Hélène looks at Léon without replying.)* O.K., let's drop it.

MAX: I have clients who are expecting merchandise. I have to know, I've been stringing them along since last month — last month! This morning one of them came to the store, he settled into a stool and refuses to budge without the remainder of his order.

HELENE: We can't all go waiting at other people's places like this, or soon we won't be able to work...

MAX: Madam, in his store he also has clients waiting, either for a wedding or a funeral... You can't make people wait indefinitely. When you set a date you have to keep your promise otherwise... Do something, Léon, we've always worked hand in hand, no?

LEON: True, but my hand is always doing the work!

MAX: I swear, if you don't deliver all the remaining merchandise by tonight, and I mean all of it, every last bit — do you hear? — then it's over between us, over!

LEON: It's over? Well then, it's over. What am I supposed to do? Cry? Hang myself?

MAX: *(his hand on his plexus)* Léon, if I ever develop an ulcer...

LEON: *(cutting him off)* An ulcer, you worry about one ulcer? I already have two — two — plus gastritis.

MAX: O.K., it's over, I can take anything, anything, except boastfulness!

LEON: *(to Hélène)* What boastfulness? He doesn't believe I'm sicker than he is?

MAX: If you would only get organized instead of working in the old Jewish way.

LEON: Aha! I see what's coming, he wants to stick us with an Aryan organizing manager! Fine, it'll be a pleasure, let him come, this time I'll leave him the keys and escape to the free zone, to the Riviera...

MAX: Why'd I get all the size forties?

LEON: *(cutting him off)* At my place that's the way it is. All or nothing!

MAX: *(continuing)* It's useless giving me all the size forties, pointless. Unless I have a bit of each size I can't deliver, I can't...

LEON: You think I'm withholding your merchandise out of sheer perversity? Huh? Deliver, deliver, what other purpose do I have in life? What other purpose?

HELENE: *(to Léon)* Léon, please. *(To Max)* We'll do our best, don't worry...

LEON: "Our best!" Take a look, take a look! *(He points to the workers.)* Every depressive, high-strung, unstable — you name it, even revolutionary — woman comes here, parks her fanny down on one of my chairs and makes believe she's working. One by one their brothers, fathers, mothers, sisters, children, husbands take turns being born, dying, getting sick. What can I do about it, huh, what?

MAX: Oh, and at my place nobody ever dies or gives birth? I'm short two warehouse men, and my bookkeeper wants to be a singer — he practices in my office and drives me nuts. Meanwhile I have to deliver item by item, run after merchandise that's doled out to me in driblets, do the bookkeeping, draw up bills, make out-of-town shipments.

LEON: Of course, but at least you sleep at night...

MAX: *(insulted)* Me, sleep at night? Me?

LEON: As soon as I close my eyes this one... *(He points to Hélène.)* pokes her elbow into my ribs. You sleeping? Of course not, and that's it, it starts. And do you remember so and so, and what about her... And by coincidence they're all dead and you can imagine how she goes on about them, and then afterwards, she cries. She has a good cry and falls asleep, but for me it's over — over — I can't sleep anymore, I get up, I go to the kitchen and I scream... I don't want to have anything to do with the dead, the dead are dead, no? And these dead are a thousand times deader than the other dead because they weren't even... Anyhow... You have to think of the living, no? And by coincidence the only close living person she still has left is me — me — and she's killing me by night while the others are murdering me by day.

Brief silence.

MAX: What's this got to do with my merchandise?

LEON: Who's talking merchandise?

HELENE: Léon, please...

Max, his fist clenched on his plexus, is suddenly writhing in pain.

LEON: Look at him, look at him, I don't believe it, he's pulling the ulcer stunt on me. If all I had were ulcers I'd be out in clubs dancing the swing every night...

MAX: Léon, seriously, let's talk man to man...

232

LEON: Right, let's talk: tell me about your fabric, what exactly is it? An unadulterated chemical synthetic special that you thought would be more stylish, huh? You think I don't know where it comes from?

MAX: It comes from Switzerland!

LEON: Right, right, it crosses Switzerland, it transits through Switzerland...

MAX: *(to Hélène)* What in the world is he driving at?

LEON: I said to myself, at least with them the delivery will be on time — never a late train, never a late convoy, the top conveyers in the world! Only for us — you and me, Monsieur Max — the fabric arrives late. Never mind, I don't say anything, whatever happens don't get worked up with these people... But when their magical unadulterated chemical fabric arrives, once it's cut and mounted, it takes on a life of its own, with a will of its own. Ask them... *(The women make a few timid remarks on the worthlessness of the fabric.)* Try ironing it, try. With a dry iron it hardens like a board and shrinks in width; with steam it shrinks in length and becomes as floppy and pleasant as a sponge; hang it up and it stretches, sags and shines. Come on, all of you, tell him... *(To the presser who nods in reply)* Come on you, tell him... And I have to oversee all this and plan!

MAX: *(yelling like a madman)* Fifty percent bonded fiber, fifty percent polyamide, the latest thing in modern technology, the latest thing!

LEON: *(in a low voice)* Right, right, the latest thing. How big a stock do they have over there, tons and tons? Ash and hair, yes sir, no use twitching your shoulders — hair, mountains of hair...

MAX: What in the world is he saying?

Léon suddenly grabs the garments from the women workers and throws them at Max's feet. Then he starts tackling the garments that are hanging. Hélène and the presser attempt to stop him and restrain him. Panic-stricken, Max picks up the garments and folds them while muttering incomprehensible words. A child appears at the doorway. He is between ten and twelve years old, wears glasses, and is hardly surprised to find the workroom in complete disarray.

MIMI: *(seeing the child, summons him)* Come in, come in...

THE CHILD: *(goes to stand directly in front of Léon then in a single breath)* My mother told me to tell you she's sorry but she won't be able to come to work today...

LEON: *(yelling like a madman)* And you come tell me this at five o'clock in the afternoon?

THE CHILD: *(not the least bit upset)* I couldn't come earlier, I had to go to the hospital.

LEON: And what about your brother?

THE CHILD: He had to go to the hospital too.

LEON: Oh wonderful, so now you both get sick at the same time, congratulations!

THE CHILD: No, it's mom.

MIMI: She's in the hospital?

234

THE CHILD: Yes.

HELENE: What's wrong?

THE CHILD: She's exhausted. She got up to come to work this morning but she was exhausted, so my brother went to get the doctor who said she had to be taken to the hospital. At the hospital they said they were keeping her under observation.

LEON: *(to Max)* Under observation. You see, you see — what can we do about it, what can we do?

MAX: Right. I'll tell my clients to tell their clients that they won't have any suits for their marriages or dances because one of your workers is under observation in the hospital.

LEON: *(yelling to Hélène)* What are you waiting for? Quick, phone in an ad. Wanted: qualified finisher, in good health, no family, no children, no interest in politics; widows, married women or divorcees need not apply. With that, maybe for once, who knows, I'll get a winner... Why are you buzzing around the kid like flies? Hell, you're here to work, right? So get to work. Take a look at them! Just look, you'd think I were already paying them by the hour...

Hélène has exited.

MAX: Léon, seriously...

LEON: Sh! No talking in front of... *(He points his chin toward the workroom. He makes Max exit and yells before exiting himself.)* No one leaves this workroom until Monsieur Max's order is ready for delivery. *(To the presser)* Meeting or no meeting...

He exits. They can be heard talking and then laughing. The women crowd around the child and bombard him with questions about Simone's health.

THE CHILD: *(shrugs his shoulder and says)* I don't know, she's tired...

MIMI: How are you going to manage, you and your brother?

THE CHILD: What do you mean?

MIMI: About eating and all that.

THE CHILD: Oh! We'll manage. I know how to cook. Lunch we eat at school anyway.

JEAN: What hospital is she in?

THE CHILD: I wrote the name of the hospital and everything on this piece of paper, it's out in the suburbs...

Mimi takes the sheet of paper.

ONE OF THE WOMEN: There you are, you kill yourself bringing up children and...

ANOTHER OF THE WOMEN: Make sure you show your mother how much you love her...

ANOTHER OF THE WOMEN: Always.

MADAME LAURENCE: I hope you're nice to her?

JEAN: Come on, leave him alone...

GISELE: Say, sweetheart, you sure have a good-looking coat. Is that the one the Americans sent you?

THE CHILD: It's not good-looking. It's a girl's coat.

MIMI: That's true: it buttons the other way. But so what? You look real handsome anyhow.

THE CHILD: I don't like it... It's a girl's coat...

GISELE: Still, the Americans are real nice sending coats to French children...

THE CHILD: I don't like the Americans.

GISELE: Why not, my lamb?

THE CHILD: I'm not a lamb, I like the Russians, the Americans want war...

The women are convulsed with laughter.

JEAN: Bravo... just for that, I'll give you a candy.

THE CHILD: I don't like candy, thank you. I better get going...

MIMI: Tell your mother to hurry back, that we'll come and visit her, and... You could kiss us goodbye before leaving, or are you already too much of a grown-up man to kiss ladies? *(The child comes back and kisses Mimi. She slips a bill into his hand which the child refuses.)* Please, buy something for yourself — and your brother.

The others also kiss him.

GISELE: Where did your mom complain it hurt?

THE CHILD: She didn't complain, she's exhausted.

GISELE: Does she still cry as often?

THE CHILD: Mom? She never cries...

MADAME LAURENCE: She'll soon be able to come back to work...

THE CHILD: *(kissing Madame Laurence)* Later on, me and my brother will work and she won't have to work ever again.

> *They all nod. The child heads for the exit.*

JEAN: What about me? I don't get kissed?

THE CHILD: Men don't kiss each other.

> *They all work diligently. Without thinking, Gisèle starts singing "White Roses".*

MIMI: Shut up!

> *Gisèle stops singing. Work continues for a moment in silence.*

GLOSSARY

Beaune-la-Rolande: An internment camp for Jews located in the Loiret. Internees were deported to Auschwitz, usually via Drancy.

Compiègne: An internment camp north of Paris, in the Oise, for Russians, French Communists and Jews. The first Jewish deportees from France left for Auschwitz from Compiègne March 27, 1942.

Demarcation line: The "frontier" between the northern zone and the southern zone of France. The North was occupied and controlled by the Germans; the southern ("free") zone was controlled by the Vichy government.

Drancy: An internment camp in a northeast suburb of Paris. First used for Jews rounded up in Paris in August, 1941, it became the main transit camp for deportations to Auschwitz and other Polish death camps. 67 convoys left Drancy between the summer of 1942 and July 31, 1944. Of the 75,721 Jews deported from French territory during the war, around 67,000 came from Drancy.

Federation: Fédération nationale des déportés, internés, résistants et patriotes. An association of former deportees, prisoners of war, members of the Resistance, and their families.

Free zone: The unoccupied part of France, controlled by the Vichy government. Following the November 1942 Anglo-American landings in North Africa, Hitler's troops crossed the demarcation line and took over all of France.

Future Brotherhood of the Sons and Daughters of Galicia: An association which sold cemetery space to people of modest means.

General Board for Jewish Affairs: Commissariat général aux questions juives (C.G.Q.J.) created in March, 1941, by the Vichy government in response to pressure from the Germans. Its purpose was to promote an antisemitic fervor in the administration and public opinion. Headed by well-known antisemites, the C.G.Q.J. directed the racial persecution of the Jews on the administrative and legislative levels, willingly adopting the same measures which the Germans had enforced in the occupied zone.

Grey mouse: Term used to designate the grey-uniformed women in the German Army.

Guingouin, Georges: Communist head of the Resistance in the Limousin region (Haute-Vienne and Corrèze).

"Hail, hail to you, brave soldiers of the seventeenth": "Salut, salut à vous, braves soldats du dix-septième". From the song "Gloire au dix-septième" by Gaston Brunschwig Montéhus (1872-1952), a singer and songwriter known for his anarchist, working class sympathies. This song made him famous; it commemorates the soldiers who refused to fire on wine growers during a 1907 uprising in the south of France.

Hipster: The French term is "zazou", a youth movement, dating from 1940, and regarded as decadent by the Vichy government. Adherents were passionately fond of American music and cultivated a special "look"—curly hair, long jackets, narrow pants and platform shoes.

Hotel Lutetia: Between April and August, 1945, many of the approximately 2,600 French deportees who survived were received in this left-bank hotel, where they were given medical checkups.

Humanité festival: An annual festival held just outside Paris by the French Communist Party; it includes performances and exhibits by international celebrities.

Immigrant Workers Movement: Main d'Oeuvre Immigrée (M.O.I.). An organization affiliated with the Communist Party. Many members were Jewish, young and daring, and participated in a number of dangerous missions organized by the Resistance.

Jewish Union: Union générale des Israélites de France (U.G.I.F.). An organization created in 1941, under the authority of the General Board for Jewish Affairs (Commissariat général aux questions juives). All French and foreign Jews were required to register with the U.G.I.F. Jewish charitable organizations were officially dissolved and placed under its aegis, but succeeded in remaining autonomous and bringing aid clandestinely, particularly in the unoccupied zone. The U.G.I.F.'s Jewish governing board struggled to provide social services for its constituency, protested against conditions in Drancy and courageously refused to collaborate with the police. In late 1943 the Vichy authorities deported the two men they themselves had appointed at its head; they perished in Auschwitz along with their wives and children. Though many Jews owe their survival to the U.G.I.F.'s services and stipends, its reputation is tainted by the fact that the Gestapo made use of their files in 1944 to deport 240 children who had been hidden in centers around Paris.

J.O.I.N.T.: American Joint Distribution Committee. Played an important role in rescuing and aiding Jews during and after the war. Within limits, the organization succeeded in discreetly supplementing limited financial resources of the Jewish Union (U.G.I.F.).

Labor Service: Service du Travail Obligatoire (S.T.O.). In order to help provide the Germans with manpower in their factories, in 1943 the Vichy government agreed to the conscription of able-bodied French workers in return for the release of French prisoners of war. The French Resistance movement was significantly reinforced by this German decision since it directly affected the French, non-Jewish, population; rather than leave for Germany, many draftees took to the hills and joined guerilla bands (the "maquis").

Laval, Pierre (1883 - 1945): Vice premier in the Vichy government in 1940, dismissed, then reinstated in 1942 with dictatorial powers.

Limoges: The administrative center of Haute-Vienne, where the Gestapo had its headquarters.

Lublin-Maïdanek: An extermination camp in Poland.

Militia and Mobile Reserve Units: Garde Mobile de Réserve (G.M.R.). These forces often supplemented those of the French police in roundups. The Militia was created by the Vichy government in January, 1943. The head, Joseph Darnand, and his men were fanatically devoted to the Gestapo; the regular police force was sometimes lax in performing its duties, but the Militia was consistently suspicious, thorough and ruthless.

Nono zone: The non-occupied or "free" zone.

O.S.E.: Oeuvre de secours aux enfants. A Jewish charitable organization for children, active during and after the war. Hundreds, possibly thousands, of children were saved by this organization. Operating covertly under the aegis of the Jewish Union (U.G.I.F.), the O.S.E. rescued children from the Vichy internment camps, placing them in centers and homes, and after 1943, evacuating them to Switzerland and Spain.

Pithiviers: An internment camp for Jews located in the Loiret. Internees were deported to Auschwitz, often via Drancy.

Ramadier, Paul (1888-1961): French political leader. A Socialist, he formed the first government of the Fourth Republic, ousting the Communists in 1947.

Royallieu-près-Compiègne: see Compiègne.

Thorez, Maurice (1900-1964): General Secretary of the French Communist Party from 1930 to his death, and minister from 1945 to 1947.

Toulouse: The administrative center of Haute-Garonne, a center of Jewish Resistance during the war.

"Tout va très bien madame la marquise": The title and refrain of a popular song by Paul Misraki, Bach and Laverne, 1936. "Everything's fine, Madam,/ Everything's fine, everything's fine,/ However I must tell you..." In the course of a telephone conversation, a valet reveals to the marquise a series of disasters that occurred in her absence — the death of her mare, the burning down of the castle and her husband's suicide. "But aside from that, Madam,/ Everything's fine..." The song was enormously popular in the troubled social and political atmosphere of the 1930's. The public probably identified with the valet's stoical black humor.

Vél d'hiv: The Vélodrome d'hiver was a large indoor sports arena near the Seine. On July 16 and 17, 1942, the French police staged a large-scale raid on the Jewish population of Paris, arresting 13,152 men, women and children ("rafle du Vél d'hiv"). Childless adults were sent directly to Drancy. The other 8,160 were taken to the Vél d'hiv where they remained for several days, in crowded and appalling conditions, before being taken to the camps of Pithiviers, Beaune-la-Rolande and Drancy. They were later deported to Auschwitz.

"White Roses": "Les Roses blanches", a sentimental 1925 song by Pothier and Raiter, made popular by Berthe Sylva. It tells of a child who steals a bouquet of white roses to give to his mother in the hospital; the saleswoman who apprehends him is so touched by his motive that she gives him the flowers; but it is too late; when the child gets to the hospital, he learns that his mother has died.